Toward a Green
Central America

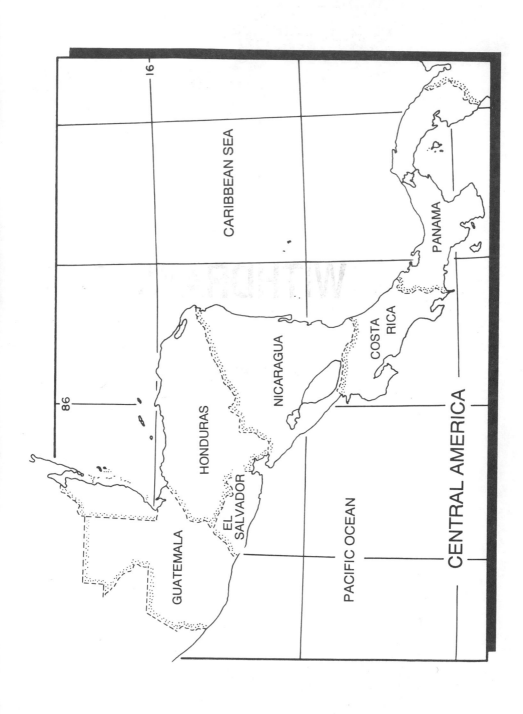

CENTRAL AMERICA

Toward a Green Central America

Integrating Conservation and Development

editors
Valerie Barzetti
Yanina Rovinski

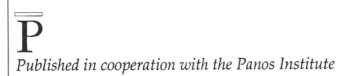

Published in cooperation with the Panos Institute

Kumarian Press

Toward a Green Central America: Integrating Conservation and Development

Published 1992 in the United States of America by Kumarian Press, Inc., 630 Oakwood Avenue, Suite 119, West Hartford, Connecticut 06110-1529 USA.

Published 1990 in Costa Rica in Spanish by Departamento Ecuménico de Investigaciones (DEI), Apartado 390–2070, Sabanilla, San José, Costa Rica, 1990.

Translated from the Spanish by David Dudenhoefer

Cover design and illustrations by Dierdre Hyde
Book design by Jenna Dixon
Maps by Alberto León
Copyedited by Jane Gold and Linda Lane-Reticker
Typeset by Sarah Albert
Proofread by Sydney Landon Plum
Index prepared by Alan M. Greenberg

Printed in the United States of America by McNaughton and Gunn.
Text printed with soy-based ink on recycled acid-free paper.

Library of Congress Cataloging-in-Publication Data

Hacia una Centroamérica verde. English
    Toward a green Central America : integrating conservation and development / editors, Valerie Barzetti, Yanina Rovinski.
       p.   cm. — (Kumarian Press library of management for development)
    Translation of: Hacia una Centroamérica verde.
    "Published in cooperation with the Panos Institute."
    Includes bibliographical references and index.
    ISBN 1-56549-006-1 (pbk.: alk.paper)
    1. Conservation of natural resources—Central America—Case studies. 2. Nature conservation—Central America—Case studies. 3. Natural resources—Central America—Management—Case studies.   I. Barzetti, Valerie, 1954– II. Rovinski, Yanina, 1960–   III. Panos Institute. IV. Series.
S934.C4H3313   1992
333.7'09728—dc20   92-9644

---

96   95   94   93   92   5   4   3   2   1
1st Printing 1992

Contents

Figures

Photographs

Foreword

Mark Halle

There can be little dissension from the observation that the notion of sustainable development has now reached an enviable level of political acceptability—a level few people would have predicted for it as recently as five years ago. The term—and to a lesser extent the concept—pervades party political platforms and adorns the publications of aid agencies and international financing institutions. Yet, like peace and justice, sustainable development is easy to accept as a goal and remarkably difficult to achieve in practice.

There are two principal reasons for this disparity. The first and more recalcitrant is that *un*sustainable development is not simply caused by poor planning, project execution, or even blinkered vision. It also arises from certain problems that are fundamental to society and to the relations between nations. Thus, for example, the fault for land degradation due to large-scale export monoculture cropping must be attributed not only to poor land husbandry practices but also to the pressures—both internal and external—that lead countries to dedicate large proportions of their best agricultural land to such practices.

The second reason for the persistence of unsustainable development resides in the fact that there is still a disturbing gap between the theory and the practice of sustainable natural resource use. It is thus with particular pleasure that I welcome the publication of this book, which presents in clear and accessible language six cases of the search for sustainable development in Central America. The case studies not only cover the different countries of the Central American isthmus, they also represent a variety of approaches to sustainable resource management and as such can serve as an excellent guide for those facing similar problems in other parts of the region and beyond.

Perhaps most gratifying, however, is the fact that the projects profiled are almost entirely designed and managed by local organizations who are taking charge of their problems and seeking solutions relying largely on their own resources. Whereas the World Conservation Union (IUCN) and other organizations have contributed in a specific technical capacity in some of the projects, all are by and large Central American initiatives, and the successes are due to their efforts.

This conclusion in itself is important. Too often the expertise and ingenuity of local and regional organizations in the developing world have been discounted or undervalued. This sad statement is unfortunately entirely applicable to Central America. I hope, therefore, that the presentation of these case studies will lead not only to a greater respect for initiatives underway in Central America but also to a realization that the rest of the world—the North included—has a great deal to learn from regions such as Central America.

Preface

Juan José Montiel
*President of the Central American Network
of Sustainable Development NGOs*
REDES

In recent years, we Central Americans have taken rapid steps to counteract the increasing destruction of our natural resources, the alteration of the environment, and the grave socioeconomic crisis that afflicts our peoples. These efforts are being made by a host of institutions that is becoming more varied every day. Nongovernmental organizations (NGOs) have become immersed in this work, and the wide spectrum of functions performed by the environmental NGOs now ranges from simple legal actions to the coordination of national and regional projects in such areas as environmental education, reforestation, watershed management, scientific tourism, community development, conservation of forests and fauna, pollution control, and even studies of the environmental impact of war.

The case studies presented in this book constitute a living example of the positive work that is being accomplished by diverse governmental and nongovernmental institutions, which often have different perspectives. These chapters especially highlight the important role the NGOs are playing within the different projects: their initiative has offered conservation alternatives that consider human needs.

The central aspects of each project are protection of water supplies, adequate use of soils, conservation of species, production of firewood, promotion of scientific tourism, and management of natural resources by indigenous communities. In each instance, success depends on two important factors: the integration and participation of local communities and the different development strategies they propose.

These cases of integrated conservation represent a great challenge. This challenge was first met with uncertainty in the decisions and solutions offered by the corresponding authorities, the acceptance or rejection of the local communities, and the socioeconomic and political situations in each country. Today these case studies serve as examples for all the countries of the area who seek to initiate a regional process of managing natural resources and integrating communities in these activities.

To conclude, as members of NGOs we are proud to be participating in these efforts toward Central American integration, which, in the near future, will prove their contribution to improving the quality of life in Central America and preserving our region's irreplaceable natural resources.

Acknowledgements

This book on integrated conservation is the result of a coordinated effort among the Panos Institute, the World Conservation Union (IUCN), and the Central American Network of Sustainable Development NGOs (REDES-CA). The six case studies presented here, as well as the introductory and final chapters, come from presentations made in February 1988 during Central America Day, in the XVII General Assembly of IUCN in Costa Rica. At that time, a team of Central American experts presented summaries of these interesting cases before more than 1,000 conservation representatives from around the world.

The great welcome the Central Americans received that day was the motivation for recovering this information and giving it a wider audience by converting it into a book that was easy to read.

Panos, IUCN, and REDES-CA wish to express their gratitude to all the people who helped make this publication possible, especially the contributors Guillermo Archibold, Rigoberto Romero Meza, Francisco Martínez Gallegos, Tamara Budowski, Lorenzo Cardenal, Manuel Benítez Arias and Juan Carlos Godoy for their valuable chapters.

A special mention goes to Stanley Heckadon, who coordinated the original presentations, contacted the authors, and contributed his own introductory chapter that places the case studies in the context of a dynamic and, at times, convulsive Central America.

We also wish to thank Gerardo Budowski, Mark Halle and Juan José Montiel for their contributions and Carlos Quesada Mateo for his summary that closes this presentation and shows the prospects for a future of conservation and development that are active and non-antagonistic.

A special recognition goes to Dierdre Hyde for contributing her artistic talent to each chapter by showing the typical art style of the respective countries. We also thank Alberto León for his maps, a task much appreciated in a region of the world where detailed maps are almost nonexistent. We would also like to thank the photographers for their contribution to the comprehension and illustration of the text.

We are grateful to the staff of the Regional Office for Central America of IUCN and the Washington office of the Panos Institute for their support and contributions. Special mention goes to Oscar Lucke and Hjalmar

Morales in Costa Rica and Patricia Ardila in Washington who, with their constant suggestions, information, and contributions, allowed us to attain the results contained in this volume.

Our special gratitude also goes to David Dudenhoefer, who translated the Spanish text without losing its flavor, and to Jane Gold for her excellent editorial input.

Finally, we are most grateful for the generous economic support of the Norwegian Development Agency (NORAD) who made possible the Central America Day presentations as well as this publication.

To all of these people our most sincere thanks.

Valerie Barzetti   Yanina Rovinski
Panos Institute   World Conservation Union/
                            Regional Office for Central America

P

About the Contributors

Valerie Barzetti is a freelance writer/editor based in Costa Rica. From January 1990 to January 1992 she directed the Central America and Caribbean Program of the Panos Institute. For the past twelve years she has worked on Central American environment and development issues and has lived and traveled throughout the region. She is a member of the International Science Writers Association, Co-op America, and Community Action on Latin America. Ms. Barzetti holds a B.Sc. in agronomy from Pennsylvania State University and a M.Sc. in agricultural journalism from the University of Wisconsin-Madison.

Yanina Rovinski is the Communications Coordinator of the Regional Office for Central America of the World Conservation Union (IUCN). She has worked throughout Central America as a freelance environmental science writer, editor, and communications consultant. She is a member of the International Science Writers Association, the Colegio de Quimico de Costa Rica, and the Colegio de Periodistas de Costa Rica. She hold a B.Sc. in chemistry from the University of Costa Rica and an M.A. in journalism from the University of California at Berkeley.

Guillermo Archibold is the director of the Management Project for the Wildlands of Kuna Yala. Between 1976 and 1982 he was the director of the Urdibi project of the Kuna Workers Union. He has written a number of publications about Kuna culture and traditions. He studied at the Agricultural School in Mandinga, San Blas, and at the National Agricultural Institute in Panama.

Manuel Benitéz Arias is the IUCN representative in El Salvador. A biologist specializing in aquatic birds, marine turtles, and coastal ecology, he worked for many years with the National Parks and Wildlife Service in El Salvador. He is a member of the International Parks Commission and the Biologists College of El Salvador. He holds a B.Sc. in biology from the University of El Salvador, where he has completed course work at the masters level.

Since 1986, **Gerardo Budowski** has served as the Director of Natural Resources at the University of Peace in Costa Rica. He also sits on the boards of the World Wildlife Fund (WWF) and the Technical Advisory Committee of the Consultative Group on International Agricultural Research. He is an honorary member of the IUCN and the Society of American Foresters. He holds an M.Sc. in forestry from Turrialba University in Costa Rica and a Ph.D. from Yale University.

Since 1984 **Tamara Budowski** has been the president of Horizontes Nature Tours in Costa Rica. Previously the sales manager of the Costa Rican Youth and Student Travel Agency, in June 1991 she received an award for distinguished service in the development of tourism in Costa Rica from the Prensa Turistica Costarricense (PRENSATUR). She studied biology at the University of Costa Rica and tourism at the University College of Cartago.

Lorenzo Cardenal is an environmentalist who has worked for the past ten years in both the governmental and nongovernmental sectors. A biologist by training, he is currently an advisor to the Nicaraguan Institute of Natural Resources (IRENA) and has served that organization in a variety of capacities. He is also an advisor to the SI/A/PAZ Project, a bi-national venture between Nicaragua and Costa Rica. He is a member of the Nicaraguan Environmental Movement (MAN).

For the past decade, **Francisco Martínez Gallegos** has been an active environmentalist in Honduras. He is currently a consultant on environmental issues for the United Nations Development Program (UNDP), specializing in environmental management for NGOs. In 1986 he coordinated the project for the development of La Tigra National Park and its buffer zone and has subsequently been a consultant to the project.

A highly respected biologist throughout Central America, **Juan Carlos Godoy** is an specialist on protected areas. He currently works on protected areas for IUCN in Guatemala. He previously worked on the protected areas project of the Center for Tropical Agricultural Research and Teaching (CATIE) in Costa Rica.

Since 1991 **Stanley Heckadon** has been a research associate at the Smithsonian Tropical Institute in Panama. From 1990–91 he served as executive director of the National Institute of Natural Renewable Resources in Panama and was the Senior Social Scientist at the Central America Tree Crop Project of the Center for Tropical Agricultural Research and Training (CATIE) from 1987–90. Mr. Heckadon received his M.A. and Ph.D. in sociology from the University of Sussex in England.

Carlos Quesada Mateo is a civil engineer with a Ph.D. in water resources systems and an M.Sc. in hydrology and natural resource planning from Colorado State University. He is presently an international consultant and a professor at the University of Costa Rica. Since 1980, he has held a number of executive and administrative positions in Costa Rica, including executive director of the Biomass Users Network and chair of the Department of Water Resources and Environmental Engineering at the University of Costa Rica.

Rigoberto Romero Meza holds a Ph.D. in forestry from Michigan State University and a masters degree in watershed management. He has over fifteen years of experience in watershed management in Honduras. He has most recently served as the executive director of the Land Use and Management Program in Honduras.

A Day for Considering Central America

Gerardo Budowski

For many who live in Europe, North America, or Asia, Central America often seems little more than a small spot on the map where some minuscule countries are located, their names and locations difficult to remember. Mention of the region evokes images of political unrest, instability, poverty, and bloody conflicts—the sad results of an unequal distribution of wealth.

Those who know the region better see past such simplifications and realize there are enormous differences among the countries—as much in the physical aspects as in the ethnic, social, and biological. The region's diversity is most marked in the area of biology: the immense richness in life forms that are concentrated on the bridge between North and South America—extraordinary fauna and flora—has for centuries been the delight of naturalists and less academic visitors.

Moreover, what few people outside the region realize is that every country boasts various conservation projects, which are run with enthusiasm, self-sacrifice, and sometimes even a greater degree of success than is found in many larger, richer tropical countries.

The following collection of six case studies was originally presented during the XVII General Assembly of the World Conservation Union (IUCN), held in Costa Rica in February 1988, where more than a thousand conservationists assembled. This collection is an attempt to make known some of the region's success stories. Though there certainly exist some similarities among their conservation accomplishments, these projects were chosen because of the diversity they reflect.

In Panama we find the extraordinary case of an indigenous organization, PEMASKY, which is representative of the country's Kuna Indians. PEMASKY is leading the efforts to keep deforestation—so common in the rest of Panama—from destroying the forests of the Kuna. The chapter's author, himself a Kuna Indian, explains that the entire community decided to declare a large part of their territory a "protected area," which allows them to keep their unique inheritance of native forest intact, preserving its exceptional flora and fauna. The community also realized they would have visitors—scientists as well as tourists—and, therefore, constructed accommodations, designed trails, and trained their people to

1

explain the secrets of their forest to the visitors.

In Honduras, the spotlight is on an exceptional area and success story for conservationists: La Tigra National Park, a cloud forest that covers a series of mountainous areas and provides drinking water for Tegucigalpa. It was not easy to convince the authorities of the need to protect the site, and pressures remain to dedicate the land to agricultural production. However, the most important step has already been taken: the park is functioning, and there is support in the capital and abroad. What is now lacking is consolidation of these accomplishments and collaboration with neighboring populations.

Costa Rica has experienced great success in the area of *ecotourism*, a term coined in that country to describe tourism based on enjoying and understanding the flora and fauna of areas visited. The development of ecotourism has not been without problems, such as tour companies trying to attract visitors by overselling attractions that are sometimes difficult to find. Despite these problems, most visitors leave satisfied with their experiences. The visits of these ecotourists provide an important source of foreign exchange for the country and are a source of pride for Costa Ricans. To develop this kind of tourism successfully, entrepreneurs have had to rely on an exceptional national parks system that is widely supported by the public—an essential requisite that exists in Costa Rica. The author of this chapter happens to be my daughter, and I would like to think that the safari trips we took with the entire family to Kenya, Tanzania, Sri Lanka, and the Canary Islands during the six years I spent as general director of the IUCN influenced her decision to dedicate herself to a type of tourism that is based on the exceptional resources of her native country, Costa Rica.

The chapter on Nicaragua describes an ambitious project to recuperate severely degraded lands in the northern Pacific region—land that has been eroded by wind and strong rains, deforested through necessity, and exploited to the point of fatigue. Dike construction, massive tree planting to create windbreaks and stabilize slopes, and the introduction of agroforestry systems—all based on the participation of groups organized from among small farmers and local and national institutions—were the focus of the Nicaraguan project.

In El Salvador we have an interesting case: the poor people who live near a lagoon are involved in efforts to recuperate a wild duck population for their conservation and use, working against the predatory customs that have threatened the birds for so long. Through well-orchestrated educational campaigns, practical reasoning, and the help of funds from abroad, the efforts have succeeded. The Salvadoran case has so much more merit when one considers that the country is passing through a tragic phase of political, social, and military convulsion. It shows that even in adverse conditions, significant advances in the field of conservation are possible.

Finally, on Guatemala's south Pacific coast, the conservation of vital ecosystems in the mangrove swamps of Monterrico has been achieved after talks and interviews won the cooperation of a fishing community and local authorities. The key to this accomplishment was an educational program that has permitted conservationists to show that, by defending the mangroves, inhabitants are defending their own local interests and can attract domestic tourism at the same time.

These are six examples of integrated conservation in Central America, much of it achieved under difficult conditions. Certainly poverty, adversity, militarization, and other problems still exist today. Many might think that, in light of so many other priorities, conservation could be placed on the back burner. That this has not been the case is due to the conservationists of Central America who have striven to integrate the needs of the population with their projects of resource preservation and recuperation. It is worth noting that many of the cases presented here could be repeated in other countries, with few adaptations necessary.

We world conservationists are thankful for the efforts of the Central Americans. Seldom have I perceived with such force the feeling of solidarity that overwhelmed the entire audience after listening to these six accounts as they were presented to the General Assembly of the IUCN. They made us feel an atmosphere of brotherhood and support. They made us feel that there is hope for Central America.

1 Central America

Tropical Land of Mountains and Volcanoes

Stanley Heckadon

Central America is a narrow strip of tropical land that is at the same time the bridge between the two continental masses of the Americas and also the isthmus that divides the planet's two largest oceans. These two factors account for its strategic value and its extraordinary biological diversity.

Comparatively, the region is small. The seven countries that constitute it cover a total surface area of only 500,000 square kilometers (approximately 193,000 square miles), which is the equivalent of a country like Spain or an island like Papua New Guinea.

Geologically, Central America is young; it did not exist 20 million years ago. At that time, a canal of ocean 3,000 kilometers (1,860 miles) in length separated North and South America and a chain of volcanic islands stretched across the gap (Figure 1.1). Then gradually, with the movements of the tectonic plates, the distance between the continents began to decrease. It is estimated that 10 million years ago, the distance had been reduced to 1,500 kilometers (930 miles), and it was barely 5 million years ago—in the recent geological past—when the Central American straits were closed and the land bridge consolidated. The last points where the two oceans remained connected were at the depression of the San Juan River Basin in Nicaragua and at the Chagres River in Panama.

The closing of the marine straits and the consolidation of the Central American land bridge constituted an important event in the climatic evolution of the planet. One effect was to alter the flow of the ocean current that, for millions of years, traveled around the world, circulating through the tropics and serving to maintain a stable global climate. In its place, two other currents were born: the Gulf Stream in the Atlantic and the Humboldt in the Pacific. These new currents initiated the great glacial periods in the Northern Hemisphere. The process of drying that created the Sahara Desert in Africa and the Atacama Desert on the Pacific coast of South America also began in that era.

Another important effect of the Central American bridge was that it permitted the "great American biological exchange." For hundreds of millions of years, North and South America had been separate continents,

5

Figure 1.1 Tectonic Evolution of Central America

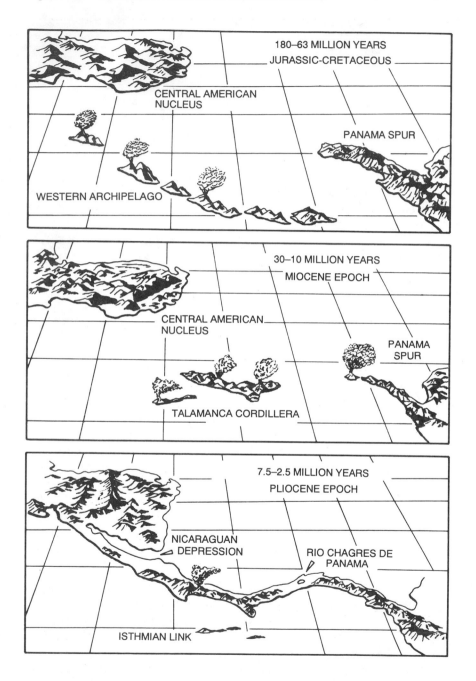

Figure 1.2   Tectonics of Central America

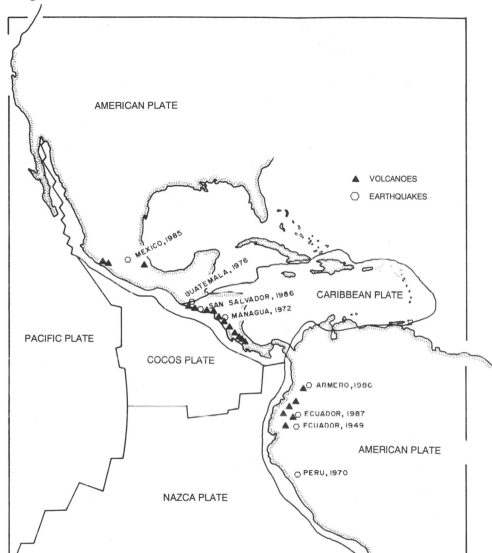

with species adapted to their own ecosystems. The isthmus now permitted species from the south to migrate to the north and visa versa.

In addition to being young, Central America is unstable, situated as it is over five tectonic plates in slow but continuous motion (see Figure 1.2). In the convergence zone between two of these plates, the Cocos and the Caribbean, there is a volcanic chain that borders the Pacific, extending from Guatemala to Panama. According to *Volcanoes of the World*,[1] sixty-eight terrestrial volcanoes have been detected there, of which more than fifteen are active in Nicaragua, four in Costa Rica, three in El Salvador, and three in Guatemala.

It is no accident that volcanoes are depicted on the flags, seals, and other symbols of the Central American nations. Their presence has a profound impression on both the land and the lives of the people. Volcanoes have simultaneously been a blessing for the fertile soils they have formed and a curse for the periodic destruction they have caused. The ancient indigenous people considered volcanic activity—or the lack of it—to presage events that would deeply affect human life and society; when the volcanoes were quiet, the mythology said, the most terrible disasters were coming. Curiously, today, when the volcanoes are more tranquil, the societies are torn by the violence of war.

Whereas the volcanoes have been quiet, seismic activity is frequent and occasionally intense. Numerous earthquakes have been devastating in terms of both economic damage and the loss of life. Guatemala City is one of the most effected metropolises; during its history, it has been severely damaged on nineteen occasions. Scanning the register of recent seismic activity, we see that in 1972 an earthquake destroyed the better part of Managua, Nicaragua; in 1976 another quake lashed the capital of Guatemala and surrounding towns; and in 1986 it was San Salvador's turn to suffer, with the estimated damage exceeding $5 million. The question is always hanging in the air: Which city will be destroyed next?

Physically, the region is mountainous, covered with wrinkles wrought by the powerful tectonic forces. Three-fourths of the isthmus is occupied by a central mountain range, that runs its entire length. This range is actually part of the same rocky spine of the Americas that extends from Patagonia to Alaska. It divides the Central American isthmus into three distinct parts: the Caribbean Slope, the Pacific Slope, and the Central Mountainous Zone. The natural and cultural differences between these regions are marked. From time immemorial, human activity has been concentrated in the Central Mountainous Zone and the Pacific Slope. Consequently, as will be discussed later, it is in these two regions that the impact of man on nature has been more strongly felt.

The location of this mountain range, perpendicular to the circulation of the winds, causes the Caribbean Slope to be more humid than the Pacific Slope. In the Atlantic, the continuous moisture-laden trade winds hit the mountain range and produce rains, leaving no real dry season. Thus, people on the Atlantic side of the isthmus say that it rains "13 months a year." For reasons that still are not clear, it also rains more the farther south one goes. The Atlantic coasts of Costa Rica and Panama are more rainy that those of Nicaragua and Guatemala. On the Pacific side, however, there are two well-defined seasons: a dry season known as summer, which can last from December until the end of April, and a rainy season commonly called winter, which can last from six to nine months, according to the area.

Figure 1.3 Soils of Central America

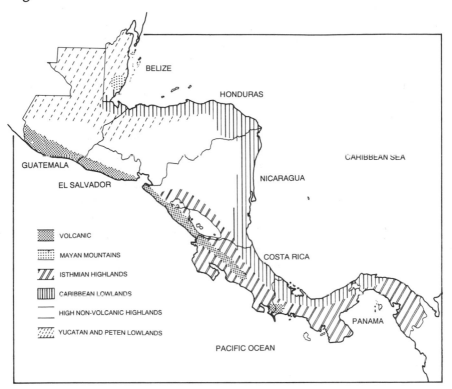

Not surprisingly, then, there is a great imbalance in the availability of surface water on the two slopes. About 70 percent of the precipitation that falls on the region runs toward the Atlantic. Those rivers, whose flows are greater and more regular during the year, drain watersheds that are wetter and cover a more extensive area. The rivers of the Pacific are shorter, contain less water, and flow more irregularly; about 90 percent of the water that runs through them falls during the short rainy season. As a result, there has been a dearth of water on the populous Pacific side, an imbalance that twentieth century populations have aggravated through deforestation of the watersheds.

Concerning temperature, which in these latitudes is best measured according to the altitude, the region can be divided into three large thermal provinces. About 60 percent of Central America is *tierra caliente,* or "hot land" (between sea level and 760 meters, or 2,500 feet); another 30 percent is *tierra templada,* or "temperate land" (760–1,830 meters, or 2,500–6,000 feet); and possibly 10 percent is *tierra fria,* or "cold land," covering areas above the tree line; in addition, there is the *tierra helada,* or "frozen land," which describes only the mountain peaks whose elevations are above 3,660 meters (12,000 feet).[2] These diverse combinations of altitude, temperature, and precipitation have given origin to some twenty vegetational provinces or regions.

Simplifying a complex reality, we could also say that the region is divided into six soil provinces: the volcanic regions, the Mayan Mountains, the isthmus highlands, the Caribbean lowlands, the nonvolcanic highlands, and the lowlands of the Yucatan and the Peten (Figure 1.3). Although the mountains have left room for only the thin coastal plains on the Pacific Slope, volcanic activity over the millennia has deposited on that slope deep and extensive layers of ash, which have contributed to the formation of some of the most fertile soil on the planet. Unfortunately, this volcanic soil is easily eroded. The Caribbean coastal plain is even more extensive, but its soil is poorer in nutrients and more acidic; moreover, because of the region's extremely high precipitation, drainage there is slower, and the soil tends to become compacted. The most fertile soil on the Caribbean plain is found along the rivers.

Along with the factors described above, there is a geopolitical characteristic that has also contributed to the sociopolitical evolution of Central America. Because of its location, the isthmus has been one of the most important routes of interoceanic travel and communication. Two countries, Nicaragua and Panama, have been most affected by this attribute. Since the sixteenth century, there have been conflicts among the world powers over control of these interoceanic routes, conflicts that have also included the Caribbean islands that neighbor the principal shipping routes leading to the Central American isthmus.

The Central American Population: Who We Are and Where We Live

There is endless debate concerning the size of the indigenous population at the time of European conquest in the early sixteenth century. The estimates fluctuate enormously, from 1 million to 10 million. What is certain, however, is that from its first contact with the Europeans, the native population declined precipitously from millions to a few hundred thousand. This demographic holocaust was due in part to diseases—the "attack forces" of the conquest —against which the Indians had no resistance. Beyond that, both the military conquest of the isthmus and the subsequent economic exploitation of the Indians were so prolonged and destructive that they wreaked havoc on the population.

During the 300-year colonial period, the population grew slowly, taking almost 100 years to double. Then, after independence in the nineteenth century, the growth rate increased slightly, although both humans and nature thwarted this demographic growth with continual wars, earthquakes, droughts, and epidemics that tore at the countries of the region.

Beginning in the twentieth century, improvements in public health, education, and living conditions spurred a demographic explosion; the annual growth rate increased three or four times to 3 and sometimes 4 percent. Thus, the time it took for the population to double was drastically reduced from 100 to 25 years. We began this century with 3 million Central Americans; in 1990 we topped 29 million, and it is estimated that by the end of the century, we will number between 35 and 40 million. This extraordinary phenomenon, which has no historic precedent, has had strong repercussions on the natural resource base and social structures. In addition, the area's population is young: 44 percent are younger than age 15.

Concerning its distribution, 50 percent of the population is concentrated on the Pacific Slope, 40 percent in the Central Mountainous Zone, and only 10 percent on the extensive Caribbean plains. Moreover, in every country the population tends to concentrate around specific areas, especially the capital cities. Panama is an extreme case, given that two-thirds live near the Canal Zone, which includes Panama City and Colón. In Costa Rica, a similar proportion lives in the plateau known as the Central Valley.

At the same time, however, the demographic transformation described above can be credited with the colonization of or—better—the migration to the jungle zones. During the first half of the present century, the agricultural frontier was found around uninhabited interior zones of the Pacific Slope. This was the case of the La Máquina and Concepción zones in Guatemala's Escuintla Department, the coastal plains of El Salvador, the region of Golfito in Costa Rica, and the Barú and Tonosí areas of Panama.

Later, and above all after World War II, thousands of campesino (peasant) families—which included people of European descent, mestizos, and indigenous groups—migrated from the most densely populated areas of the Pacific Slope and Central Mountainous Zone toward the rain forest zones, situated for the most part on the Caribbean Slope. Currently, the colonization front extends for thousands of kilometers along the entire length of the isthmus, from Belize to "Costa Arriba" of Colón in Panama. Only in Nicaragua was the intensity of colonization diminished by the war.

Among the many consequences of the colonization, two are worth pointing out. One is ecological: the deforestation caused by the thousands of families who migrated from the drier zones to the moist forest zones, bringing with them their traditional methods of production based on slash-and-burn agriculture and extensive cattle ranching. The second one concerns social order: the colonists, usually mestizos (persons of mixed European and native ancestry), invade areas traditionally occupied by the ethnic minorities of the Atlantic, populations that are generally black or indigenous. Unfortunately, in the repeated conflicts that have arisen from this migration, the national authorities have tended to intervene in favor of the immigrants, who they consider to be carriers of the so-called national culture.

Central America's greatest treasure is its people. In his excellent essay "The Indian That We Nicaraguans Carry Within Us," Pablo Antonio Cuadra takes up the theme of Nicaragua's cultural and ethnic roots. We could apply his metaphor to the entire region, amplifying it to include the Indian, white, and black that we Central Americans carry within us.

Pre-Columbian Central America was culturally divided into two areas: one, the nucleus of the high cultures, densely populated and located in the fertile volcanic soils of the highlands and the Pacific Slope; the other, a less populated area that was located on the rainy Atlantic zones of what is now Costa Rica and Panama and was inhabited by more primitive tribes. With the conquest of the Indians and the introduction of the white and black peoples, however, racial mixing became a powerful social factor. Central America today is, above all, a mestizo region—a heterogenous mosaic of ethnic, linguistic, and cultural groups. (For example, twenty-six indigenous languages are spoken in Guatemala alone.)

However, it has been difficult for us to understand and evaluate this extraordinary cultural diversity. One constant in the national politics of the dominant groups has been an attempt to erase these differences and standardize all the variations of the cultural topography. We have tended to depreciate the valuable contribution of the Native American and the African to the configuration of our current societies. But it is precisely in the acceptance of the cultural differences and the mutual respect among groups that our societies are strengthened and given a greater identity.

The Central American Economy

Those who have studied the economic history of the resource-rich Central American nations have characterized them as "agro-export" economies. The central theme of this history is known as the search for an "impulse product," a crop whose exportation would generate wealth. Since the sixteenth century, these economies have been oriented toward monoculture, a dependence on volatile external markets, and consequently, alternating cycles of booms followed by crashes and depression. Also early on was the orientation of the societies toward the Pacific while the markets were located on the Atlantic.

How We Earn Our Living

From colonial times, most of the population was found at the base of the social pyramid, living in an economy of subsistence. On the other hand, most of the wealth and sociopolitical power in Central America was concentrated in the export products. During the first decades of the sixteenth century, it was the mining of gold and the sale of slaves that brought the first wave of prosperity. Following that period came the first agricultural bonanza, based on cacao and occupying the best volcanic soils of the Pacific. The principal market was then located in Mexico. Cultivation of cacao expanded through Guatemala, El Salvador, Honduras, Nicaragua, and, to a smaller degree, Costa Rica. This boom ended because of a scarcity of workers and the competition from Ecuadorean and Venezuelan cacao.

Throughout the seventeenth and eighteenth centuries, the bulk of the wealth came from the cultivation and extraction of indigo. This industry first prospered until the fall of the Spanish economy in the early eighteenth century; it prospered again toward the end of that century with the expansion of the textile industry in Northern Europe, only to crash forever with the discovery of synthetic dyes in 1856.

In the 1850s, a true social and economic revolution took place with the introduction of the cultivation of bananas and coffee. This economic power continued until the Great Depression of the 1920s. It is difficult to understand the current societies without making reference to the role of the banana plantations and coffee farms.

Coffee occupied the best volcanic soils; banana, the fertile alluvial soils of the great rivers, initially on the Atlantic Coast, but later in large areas of the Pacific Coast. Since these were sparsely populated zones, labor had to be imported. From the Antilles, thousands of workers, the vast majority of whom were black, Protestant, and English speaking, were brought to the plantations of the Atlantic Coast. They also contributed to the cultural and ethnic diversity of the region. This migration was not limited to the Antilleans; the waves of Salvadoran workers were also large.

The extraordinary dispersion of these crops was made possible by the transportation revolution. The train and steamship permitted the cheap and speedy shipment of these crops to foreign markets. In the entire region, there were big investments in roads, train lines, and docks to link the centers of production with the docks of embarkation.

The ways societies were organized around these crops varied, just as did their social and political effects. In Costa Rica, the cultivation of coffee was centered on the small farmer. Some researchers have suggested that this early orientation toward economic democracy formed the basis for the rise of Costa Rican political democracy. On the other hand, in Guatemala and El Salvador, the coffee riches were concentrated in large plantations, which replaced small subsistence farms and forced the small farmer to labor for someone else, unable to make a profit. In a similar way, the banana industry also contributed to the vast impoverishment of Central American campesinos. This economic inequality did not make fertile soil for political equality.

In the years following World War II, the agro-export economies became more diversified. Coffee and bananas were joined by cotton, sugar, and beef. From 1950 to 1970, cotton plantations expanded along the southern coast of the isthmus. From Guatemala to Costa Rica's Guanacaste province, the cultivation of cotton led to the rapid disappearance of the dry forests. In El Salvador, cotton expansion, combined with the construction of a coastal highway, caused the destruction of the last 300,000 hectares (741,000 acres) of dry forest that remained in the country. In all of Central America, the deforested zones with the most serious forestry needs today are the cotton-producing areas. Moreover, whereas the cultivation of coffee replaces an upland forest with a new ecosystem of coffee bushes and shade trees, the cotton plantation is an unstable ecological system, a monoculture that requires lowland soil and vast amounts of chemicals to combat insects. Thus, in addition to rapid deforestation, the cultivation of cotton also triggered an intense conflict between people and insects.

When the North American market was closed to Cuban sugar in the 1960s, the Central American sugar industry underwent an immediate and substantial expansion. It required the construction of large and more modern sugar mills, an activity that tended to be concentrated on the Pacific Slope.

From colonial times, cattle ranching was an important activity centered in the dry lands of the isthmus. Beginning in the 1950s, the growing urban demand for beef in all the countries, along with the opening of new foreign markets, gave a strong boost to the cattle industry. International loans contributed greatly to the expansion of pastures at the cost of forests. During the 1980s, 65 percent of the agricultural land was covered by extensive cattle ranches; of the rest, export crops represented 16 percent, and land dedicated to basic grains and other food crops represented 19 percent.

Our Current Economic Crisis

The three decades after World War II were years of economic boom and social transformation. All indicators showed a period of substantial economic growth in Central America amounting to almost 4 percent annually, a higher rate than in the rest of Latin America. This growth promoted industrialization, and considerable resources were invested in works of basic infrastructure.

This period also saw improvement in almost all social indicators. The Central Americans increased their life expectancies while rates of mortality and illiteracy dropped. The societies became more complex as a middle class appeared, practically nonexistent before World War II. In general, all the studies of the period indicated a progressive improvement in earnings and quality of life.

Suddenly, at least in historical terms, beginning with the oil shortage of 1973, the region sank into a period of economic depression and social dislocation, that has continued to the present. We are witnessing the growing impoverishment of large strata of the population. There is an

Figure 1.4   Distribution of Farmland in Central America, 1975

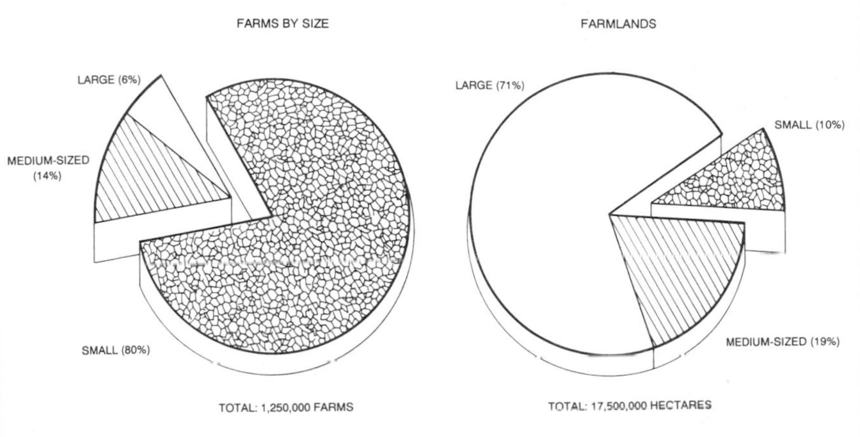

FARMS BY SIZE

FARMLANDS

LARGE (6%)

MEDIUM-SIZED
(14%)

SMALL (80%)

TOTAL: 1,250,000 FARMS

LARGE (71%)

SMALL (10%)

MEDIUM-SIZED (19%)

TOTAL: 17,500,000 HECTARES

increase in what can be called "structural poverty": there are more poor every day, and each day the poor grow poorer.

The gross domestic product of the countries has fallen to the level of the 1960s. The wealth available to each Central American has diminished; the income of the region's inhabitants is less than what it was 20 years ago. Food production is falling and the list of countries that import food, which includes basic grains such as corn, rice, and beans, grows daily. Whereas Costa Rica, for example, was once practically self sufficient, it now imports a considerable quantity of food. Unemployment and underemployment have acquired new magnitudes, especially for the rural population such as the small farmer and the farmer without land for whom unemployment tends to be permanent.

Internal and external factors have combined to cause this crisis. During the period of economic growth, there was a great concentration of land ownership. In 1976 there were 1,250,000 farms or agricultural projects in the region, which together comprised some 18 million hectares (over 44 million acres, or 69,000 square miles). As Figure 1.4 indicates, farms smaller than 10 hectares (25 acres), which represented 80 percent of the total, controlled only 10 percent of the land while those larger than 200 hectares (494 acres), which represented barely 8 percent of the farms, comprised a region that was almost 70 percent of the area in use. The number of families without land is also increasing, as is the number of those who have parcels so small, called *minifundia*, that they do not permit food self-sufficiency. Generally, the rural poor tend to occupy land that is both marginal and fragile, land that is usually suitable for nothing other than forestry.

Among the external factors is a profound dilemma in the global economy: the lack of justice, as it could be called, in the exploitative relationship between the industrialized countries and those that, like the Central American nations, live off their agricultural exports. It should be noted that our export products are worth less every year while the prices of the manufactured goods we import increase. Every year we have to sell more tons of bananas, sugar, or coffee to buy the fertilizers or tractors used in production. Additionally, all the Central American nations are deeply indebted to credit institutions—public and private—of the developed nations. The external debt exceeds $40 billion. The interest that should be paid annually has risen to disturbing amounts. In the case of Panama, where the debt exceeds some $5 billion, this interest is approaching $400 million annually. The stability of the tropical ecosystems of the isthmus depends on how this inequality is addressed.

Politics, War, and the Economy

To conclude, it is necessary to point out that those who study our ways of governing characterize us as traditional, authoritarian states. To its own misfortune, Central America has long opted for a pattern of government that is authoritarian and centralized, with power concentrated in few hands—frequently those of political bosses and military leaders. This long-standing strongman tradition has generated an authoritarian, politically intolerant culture. Dissension can cause one to be catalogued first as seditious and later as subversive.

Since the 1970s, violence has increased. Currently, there are 1.5 million armed men in the region, including armies, guerrillas, and support groups for the warring factions. For a region of 25 million inhabitants, this figure represents an exaggerated proportion of armed people—perhaps the highest in the world today. The deaths caused by war have reached almost 200,000 while the wounded number approximately 400,000. In addition, such violence has created more than 3 million Central American refugees, both within the region and beyond. Thousands of refugees have emigrated to Mexico, the United States, and, lately, Australia.

The resultant flight of capital has been enormous. Moreover, while the financial and physical costs of this violence in such countries as El Salvador, Nicaragua, and Guatemala have yet to be estimated, they may be equivalent to the foreign debt. Beyond all the monetary costs, we must endure an enormous moral load: the disintegration of families and the cracking of moral values due to the violence. Undoubtedly, many years must pass before these wounds will heal.

Given these difficult political and economic circumstances, it is understandable that the main priorities of the population focus on security—specifically, employment, nourishment, and personal safety.

The Environmental Impact of Our Type of Development

The cosmology of the ancient Indians held that order arose out of harmony and equilibrium among the gods, nature, and man. Yet the mestizo culture of Central America, strongly influenced by Judeo-Christian principals, operates on the premise that nature exists for humans to conquer at any cost. This is their traditional way to view the natural world. The myth shared by the inhabitants of the region is that our natural resources are inexhaustible and that we can therefore use them and even abuse them, forgetting about the price we will have to pay later for such recklessness. Fortunately, one can already see positive signs of change in the vision of our modern societies toward the natural world around us, visions that are again approaching the ancient indigenous cosmology.

Current strategies for economic and social development of the countries in the region, formulated during the 1960s and 1970s, speak of the urgency and necessity of "incorporating the jungle into the national economy." They consider the tropical forests to be an obstacle to development and a symbol of national backwardness. Deemed uncultivated wastelands, the forests have to be replaced. In other words, the forests are not thought to provide any benefit.

In our region, the most radical transformation that economic development has brought has been the unprecedented destruction of the forests. In 1950, three-quarters of Central America was still covered with forest. Today this situation is almost inverted: there now remains only 30 percent of forest cover in the area (Figure 1.5). This devastation affects all types of forest—dry and wet, upland and lowland. It is estimated that the annual rate of deforestation is 376,000 hectares (almost 1,450 square miles) during normal years. When there is a drought and the summer expands from three or four months to six or seven, destruction can reach 400,000 hectares (almost 1,550 square miles). At this rate, the forests that survive to the year 2000 will be isolated patches in biogeographical islands, in the highlands or most inaccessible zones of the Caribbean Slope or within the systems of national parks subject to protection. Understandably, most of the forests that will remain standing in the year 2000 are today inhabited by ethnic minorities who use production systems and enjoy lifestyles that are in harmony with the environment.

If we compare the area that we cut with that which we reforest, the disparity is alarming. In all the countries combined, we plant barely 70,000 hectares (173,000 acres) per year. But this number is unreliable because it refers to the area planted, half of which is unlikely to survive due to lack of maintenance and financial resources.

The main factors in this immense transformation are land use and expansion of the agricultural frontier. Those mostly responsible for it are the thousands of campesino families with little or no land who migrate from the densely inhabited and degraded areas to the jungle zones to

Figure 1.5   Deforestation in Central America

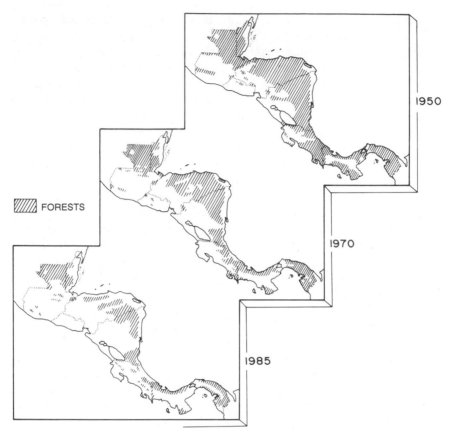

colonize the forest. Despite great technological advances within the agro-export sector (cotton is a typical example of high-tech agriculture), these farmers remain largely outside the credit system and lack access to technical assistance. Thus, most of them continue to use the traditional technology of the axe, machete, and fire. With these tools, the peasants first destroy the forest to plant basic grains; then, when the soil loses its limited natural fertility, they plant pasture for cattle. In a few years, the small farms are mostly occupied by pasture for cattle ranching.

When the demographic densities are low, these methods of agriculture are adequate. With an increase in the population, however, the same methods turn destructive and break mankind's equilibrium with the natural resources. To the extensive deforestation is added the loss of soils and their compaction.

Nor are the drawbacks of cattle ranching solely ecological. As practiced in Central America, small-scale cattle ranching does not provide most campesinos with enough money to survive. Using current systems, 20 to

30 hectares (about 50–75 acres) of pasture are not economically profitable. Moreover, the annual burning of pastures, overgrazing by cattle, and degradation of soils by compaction or erosion contribute to the low productivity: only some 33 pounds of meat per hectare per year. Thus unable to sustain their families with the meager income ranching brings, many campesinos sell their properties to large ranchers, beginning a process called "neo-latifundism": at the colonization front, small and medium-sized producers appear first, but later the land is concentrated in only a few hands; the cattle zones generate little employment and eventually expel populations.

Whereas the destruction of forests is closely linked to the expansion of the agricultural frontier on the Atlantic coast, the factors are different on the Pacific Slope and in the Central Mountainous Zone. Here, where the bulk of the population is found, pressure on surviving forests is aggravated by the growing demand for firewood for both domestic and industrial consumption. Three-quarters of the Central American population use wood for energy. The per capita firewood consumption is about one cubic meter per year, and the number of consumers is about 20 million. At the same time, a growing number of small and medium-size rural industries depends on firewood to process their products. Throughout the region are thousands of saltworks, brickworks, lime kilns, and charcoal kilns. All told, more than half the energy consumed in the region comes from firewood; in comparison, hydroelectric energy provides barely 5 percent and imported petroleum, 37 percent.

One dilemma created by the current strategies for economic and social development is how to satisfy the energy demands of rural industry without destroying the last upland forests, where the watersheds for the cities of the Pacific Slope originate. On that slope, the cities are confronting serious problems with the water supplies for their populations and industries. In nearly all the cities, and especially in capitals such as Tegucigalpa, Managua, San Salvador, and Guatemala City, large sectors are continuously short of water, and some neighborhoods have running water for only a few hours a day, one or two days per week. As it has been said: "We are becoming a dry and thirsty continent."

Another grave problem caused by the disappearance of the forests from steep areas is the loss of soil—Central America's principal natural resource. This degradation especially affects the countries on the Pacific Slope, the worst case being El Salvador, with 45 percent of the soil degraded, while scarcely 2 percent of the soil in Belize has been lost. (Although the territory of both countries is similar [22,000 square kilometers, or approximately 8,500 square miles], El Salvador has 5.2 million inhabitants whereas Belize has only 180,400.) Central America is not compensated for the soil that ends up year after year in the ocean. Worse, the land that does not make it to the ocean causes sedimentation in the reservoirs of hydroelectric dams, reducing the life spans of these expensive projects.

Still another tragedy caused by encroaching deforestation is what promises to be the massive extinction of the complex and diverse tropical fauna and flora. Their disappearance will mean the loss of unique genetic materials vital to medical and agricultural advancement.

Compounding these problems is a tendency in Central America, especially in the agro-export sector, to overuse agrochemicals, many of which are highly toxic. Increasingly, this practice is contaminating the soil and water and, worse yet, is poisoning life. In the urban zones, industrialization and urbanization cause such problems as water pollution and accumulation of garbage. All the cities dump their untreated sewage into rivers or lakes or off the nearest coast. In this manner, Nicaragua destroyed Lake Managua, Panama did the same with the Bay of Panama, Guatemala destroyed Lake Amatitlán, and El Salvador ruined the Acelhuate River and the Cerrón Grande Reservoir.

In Central America, history has shown the consequences of misguided development. To combat the deleterious effects of this development, plans were conceived with the sole purpose of conserving natural resources. The six projects described here were developed in response to those original plans and reflect some of the efforts that are now under way in Central America to inject people back into the conservation formula. This innovation of the conservationist programs has resulted from the need to attend to the demands of the communities that live within the areas covered by the plans, as well as in surrounding zones, so as to obtain their collaboration.

If we continue on the path we have followed thus far, a discouraging future awaits us. The hour has arrived for us to seek a new direction, one that respects the inherent harmony of nature and leaves open options for future generations. It is the same path the indigenous people of Central America have followed for centuries.

Notes

1. Tom Simkins, *Volcanoes of the World* (Stroudsberg, Penn.: Hutchinson Ross Publishing Co., 1981), 90–95.
2. Robert C. West, *Middle America: Its Lands and Peoples*, 3d ed. (Englewood Cliffs, N.J.: Prentice-Hall, Inc., 1989), 40–41.

2 Pemasky In Kuna Yala

Protecting Mother Earth . . . And Her Children

Guillermo Archibold

> The Earth is our mother and also our culture. In her, the
> elements of our culture are born: the leaves we use in the
> ritual ceremonies of puberty, all the food we consume in the traditional
> festivals, the materials that our artisans use and that we use to construct
> our houses all come from the forest. If we were to lose these lands, there
> would be no culture, and there would be no people. (Leonidas Valdez,
> second general chief of Kuna Yala)[1]

We Kuna are a nation of more than 30,000 people who have always made
our living from the forest and the sea. Our population is distributed today
over fifty island communities along the entire Atlantic coast of Panama.
For us, both the sea where we live and the forest that covers the steep
Kuna Yala Mountain Range are our grocery stores, our pharmacies, our
source of life. We take what we need from them: medicine, food, and
fresh water. In addition, our sacred objects come from the forest, which is
the home of the spirits. The spirits' home must be respected; if not, their
anger could bring sickness and disgrace to the Kuna people. Therefore,
we Kuna must care for our territory, from the heights of the mountains to
the depths of the sea.

In 1970 when the government of Panama began the construction of the
Llano-Cartí road from the Chepo Plain to the coast at Cartí (Figure 2.1),
we Kuna leaders felt that the cultural and territorial integrity of our
people was threatened. From the beginning of the road's construction,
deforestation increased in our region, as did poaching and the extraction
of forest products. Colonists began to arrive from the country's interior,
looking for the land they needed to survive. They cut and burned the
forest to plant crops that, after a short while, did not produce well
anymore. As the land became exhausted, the colonists sold it or planted
pasture and brought in cattle. The road also facilitated the arrival of
certain members of the powerful upper classes. All along the mountain
range that separates our district from the Panama province, the jungle,
which had been verdant with great biological diversity, was rapidly being
transformed into a desolate land with neither trees nor animals. Faced
with this threat, we Kuna began our efforts to exercise some control over
the immigration of colonists to our lands, efforts that continue to this day.

21

The Pemasky Plan

In 1975, a group of young volunteers from the Kuna Workers of the Canal Area (AEK), in an attempt to confront the accelerated immigration of colonists, created a small experimental agricultural colony in Udirbi, at the point where the road enters the region. The group initially planted cassava, corn, bananas, and sweet potatoes—crops that did not do well. They then tried perennials such as coffee, cacao, cashew, and peach palm (*pejibaye*). These crops did not adapt well to the rain and cold of the zone, either. The volunteers also tried to raise pigs, chickens, and cattle—and also failed.

In 1981, worried by such discouraging results, the AEK began to consult forestry specialists from various national and international institutions, looking for alternative ways to ensure the Kunas' permanence on the mountain range.

In 1983, the Udirbi project gained new vigor with the assistance of the Tropical Agricultural Center for Research and Education (CATIE) and the Smithsonian Tropical Research Institute (STRI), and with financial support from the Inter-American Foundation (IAF), the U.S. Agency for International Development (USAID), the World Wildlife Fund (WWF), the MacArthur Foundation, and some national institutions. With this help a study of the region's natural and cultural resources was undertaken. It then served as the basis for the development of a management plan for the zone,[2] which includes the Study and Management Project for the Wildlands of Kuna Yala (PEMASKY).

The goal of the PEMASKY plan is both the organization of natural resources use via conservation of Kuna Yala's terrestrial and marine ecosystems and the protection of the cultural and historical values of the Kuna people. The plan requires that the region's natural resources be managed in a sustainable manner to ensure their use for the benefit of the community. The plan also recommends promoting scientific research, environmental education, and nature tourism while respecting the cultural norms of the Kuna people.

The World of the Kuna People

The Kuna Vision of Nature

Upon studying the management plan, it becomes evident that the knowledge of the Western scientists coincides with the Kunas' vision of nature, although our beliefs stem from very different reasoning. We Kuna consider that any type of threat to a part of the region is a threat to our territory and survival. If Mother Nature were destroyed, we would lose our culture and spirit. In the words of our thinkers:

Figure 2.1 Management Project for the Wildlands of Kuna Yala

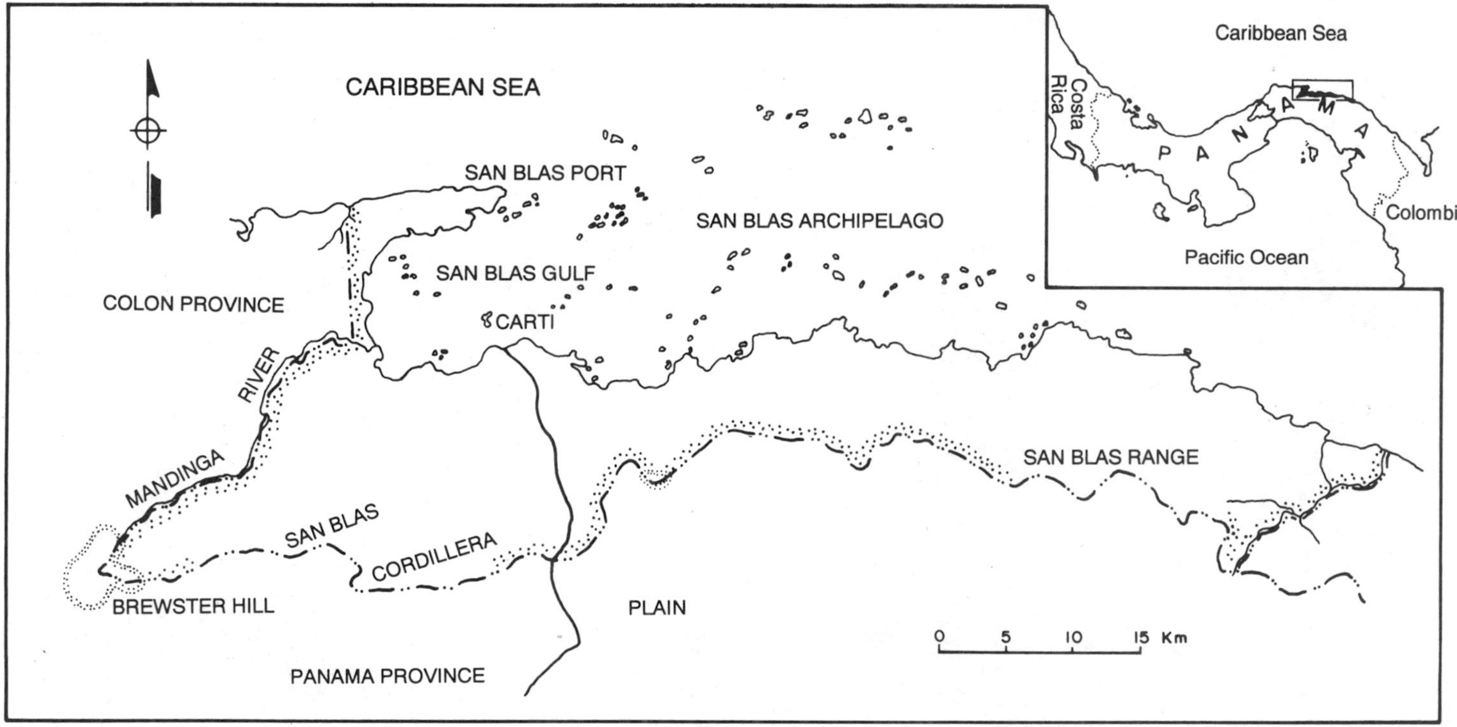

Some areas of the jungle are sacred: whirlpools, trees, crags, etc., belong to spirits prone to fury. The alteration by human beings is converted into violence against the community that disturbs their domain. (A Kuna)

The great resources, the mines of gold, iron, copper, coal, and elements like nitrogen, phosphorous, potassium, and others, are the internal organs of Mother Earth. The pulse and heartbeat of Mother Earth produce the trees and plants for food, clothing, homes and medicine for all beings of the Earth. Therefore, the entrails of the Mother shouldn't be abused and mistreated. (A Kuna)

In Kuna philosophy and religion, all of nature that Pab Dumad (God) created has its own life; it feels and listens. Mankind and nature are friends and companions who mutually help each other. The Great Mother supplies all the needs of present and future generations; thus, the death of one species means the extinction of another.

Such beliefs and knowledge of nature are commented upon almost daily in our local congresses and when we gather each night, as is our custom, to discuss problems, resolve conflicts, make decisions, plan our work, and pass on our traditions.

A Lush Storehouse of Natural Resources

Kuna Yala, in the San Blas district, is situated on the Atlantic coast of Panama. It is a rough and irregular region. The district comprises the San Blas Mountain Range, San Blas Point, the Gulf of Mandinga, and numerous coral islands. Its 3,208 square kilometers (1,240 square miles) extend from the heights of the Kuna Yala Mountain Range to the white sands of the Caribbean, from Colón province 375 kilometers (233 miles) south to the border with Colombia. The highest point in the mountain range is Brewster Hill (Cerro Brewster, or *Diamma Yala*), 910 meters (2,985 feet) above sea level.

On the mountain range's Atlantic slope are the sources of the Mandinga, Cangandí Nergala, Acua, Gardi Dumman, Gardi Seni, and Nuu rivers. More than 300 islands and rocky crags dot the region's crystalline waters, where yachts, sailboats, and ocean liners appear on the horizon every day, attracted by the beauty of the reefs, the beaches, and the culture and handiwork of the Kunas.

In its first phase, PEMASKY concentrated on the western part of the region in the municipality of San Blas—an area covering about 115,000 hectares (444 square miles), excluding the marine area and buffer zone. Annual precipitation in the Nusagandi zone, the project site, is approximately 3,500 millimeters (137 inches).

A humid region covered with exuberant tropical forests, Kuna Yala contains four life zones: tropical moist forest, tropical wet forest, tropical premontane moist forest, and tropical premontane rain forest. Whereas in the high parts of the mountain range the climate is humid and cold (*ami*),

Photo 2.1   The Llano-Cartí road: The Llano-Cartí road connects the community of Kuna San Blas with the rest of the world. However, it also brings colonists, grazing, stress to the land, and deforestation. *Credit: Mac Chapin, IAF*

the coast and lowlands are humid and warm (*awi*). These climate types have given rise to diverse and dense vegetation, which the Kunas know well and have traditionally used. Many species that were discoveries for the Western scientists had been well known by the Kuna for centuries. One such plant is *akepandup*. Ten years ago, scientists reported having discovered this spiny vine, which they baptized *Randia pepoformis*; however, the Kuna had been using it to cure many sicknesses for thousands of years. Similarly, botanists believed until 1985 that *sapi garda* (*Simaba polyphylla*), which the Kunas use to stimulate intelligence, was found only in Brazil. Another plant that is well known to the Kunas is *irasgui*, which the scientists discovered in 1977 and named *Tachigalia versicolor*. This tree flowers and fruits only once and then dies. We do not use it because one who uses it will die young, or when his descendants are born, they will die.

Thus it is that

> the Kuna botanists know the functions and importance of each plant and the influences of its curative powers, which man can apply for his well being and benefit. When they make use of the bark of a medicinal tree, they extract it with great delicacy, removing each piece following the position of the four cardinal points—a piece from the north, one from the south, east, west. (A Kuna)

There is also a great richness of fauna in the Kuna territories, both aquatic and terrestrial. The forests of the mountain range are the home of innumerable birds, such as toucans, owls, hummingbirds, hawks, eagles, curassows, and parakeets. Snakes, which cause such fear among city dwellers, are habitual guests on Kuna land; boas, coral snakes, rattlesnakes, and the fearsome fer-de-lance abound here. Other reptiles, such as iguanas, ctenosaurs, and chameleons, also live in the foliage.

Perhaps most attractive for both the Kunas and their visitors are the mammals found within the jungle. From the lush canopy of the trees sound the calls of the howler monkeys. More quiet are the felines— jaguars, pumas, ocelots, and margays. Also hidden there are deer, rabbits, peccaries, and pacas—traditional food for the local inhabitants. Other forest marauders include raccoons, opossums, tapirs, porcupines, and sloths.

The waters of the rivers are inhabited by caimans, turtles, frogs, and toads. There are also some fifteen species of freshwater fish, some of which are important for the local diet. Where the rivers pour into the ocean, one finds thousands of brightly colored fish that live around the coral reefs. With their varied sizes and unique colors, these inhabitants of the sea are the reason many skindiving enthusiasts travel to the area. Other species, such as sea turtles, lobster, shrimp, and sea cucumbers, complete the marine fauna.

Photo 2.2 Kuna Hunter: For the Kunas, the forest is the source of food, medicine, and construction material. *Credit: Carlos Gomez*

Government, Economy, and Social Dynamics

The region is governed by its own social, political, and cultural struc-
ture—an autonomy that the government of Panama has recognized since
February 1953. The 30,000 inhabitants of the district's 50 island communities are organized by their own administrative norms. Each community
has *sailas* (authorities) who, together with a group of collaborators,
administer all activities and direct the development of the village. The
maximum authority of the entire territory rests in the General Kuna
Congress, which convenes every six months and in which all delegates
and *sailas* from each community participate. Three general chiefs preside
over the Congress and are responsible for seeing that all accords and
decisions are applied.

The fundamental basis of the economy in the entire Kuna district is
subsistence agriculture on small parcels of land. Yet the activity that earns
the most money in the agricultural sector is the production of coconuts,
which are shipped to Colombia, followed by production of bananas and
plantains. To increase their incomes, families also capture fish and lobster,
and they make and sell *molas* (the typical dress of Kuna women, made
from fragments of material). However, touristic activities, cottage industries, the sale of fuel, and income from professional services are becoming
more important every day.

From the time that our ancestors arrived on the coasts of San Blas, we
Kunas have always used the sea to reach neighboring communities and to
travel beyond our territory. Today, we also use the air to travel to Panama
City, as well as the Llano-Cartí road—the only available route by land.
Since 1979, the Kuna communities have also enjoyed a radio communication network, which is used to exchange messages and information. They
have even begun to install public telephones in the most important communities, using microwave systems.

Many villages have plumbing, power plants, health centers, business
centers, and airports, and on some islands, government offices operate.
Thus, constant coordination with the national government is maintained,
although the dynamics of social development are practically independent.

Pemasky: Traditional Wisdom and Modern Science

Combining cultural beliefs and traditions with the modern conservation
techniques developed by scientists, the PEMASKY project includes scientific research, personnel training, appropriate agriculture, and supervi-
sion, all geared toward ensuring the region's protection. To facilitate this
protection, PEMASKY recommended to the Kuna General Congress that
its territory be managed as a biosphere reserve. The Congress approved
the proposal in November 1987, during a meeting in Achudup. Since

then, based on the general plan for the management and development of the district of the Kuna Yala Biosphere, the region has been divided into management zones, defined according to their ecological characteristics.

Among PEMASKY's activities, one of the most important is scientific research. In addition to the colonists, scientists have been arriving in the district since the way was opened by the Llano-Cartí road. For the most part, they have been botanists, interested in the region's exuberant flora. Since their arrival, approximately twenty new species and two genera (*Sanblasia* and *Reldia*) of plants have been discovered in the district. In the beginning, these discoveries were not shared with the Kuna community. Thus, the project decided to demand the constant participation of Kuna co-researchers in any project of scientific investigation.

With time, we decided that our people should participate not only in the area of scientific research but also directly in the planning of resource management. This collaboration does not only favor the Kuna; the Western technicians have also seen their vision enriched by our concepts and traditional knowledge.

In addition to the research program, PEMASKY intends to strengthen traditional farming methods, combining ancient wisdom with modern techniques. Such methods include alternating fruit and hardwood trees with annual crops and giving the land a rest period to restore its fertility. When a parcel is fallow and covered with thickets, we know that it is taking its medicine from Mother Earth and that in a few years it will recover its strength to give us fruit again. This system of forest-agriculture-fallow is a continuous cycle of regeneration that permits the soil to remain always covered with a layer of vegetation while the farm continues producing different products.

Close Encounters of the Third Kind

Although we Kuna have for the most part conserved our cultural identity, there are more external influences that daily and systematically affect the routine of our lives. Our economy, which has always been based on group work and cooperation, is becoming more individualistic, oriented toward business and the acquisition of money to buy food and other consumer products. An exodus toward the city has also begun, especially among our young people. Although their leaving causes us pain, many of these young people become professionals who, in keeping with their respect for tradition, collaborate with us in our activities here.

Just as the city attracts our young people, the beautiful islands and beaches of Kuna Yala regularly attract thousands of visitors. The tourists bring money into the region, but they also bring problems. Their growing presence in the zone increases the pressures on our resources and creates

Photo 2.3 Tourist Boat: Large numbers of tourists regularly visit the Kuna Yala district. They bring money, but they also leave their mark on the culture, traditions, and natural resources of the region. *Credit: Carlos Gomez*

new sources of pollution, which the fragile ecosystem is not prepared to absorb.

The typical clothing of our women, the *molas*, are so attractive that a strong demand for them has arisen, generating a cottage industry in their production. To supply the tourists, Kuna women have organized themselves into a cooperative of 1,500 members, which last year sold more than $100,000 worth of goods to Panamanians as well as to the rest of the world. Although this income represents a great benefit for our people, such volume endangers the quality of the *molas*. Thus, it was decided to provide courses for the artisans to help them maintain the quality of their products and keep them from losing respect for our traditions and culture.

Education is also important to the Kunas. There are elementary schools in almost all our communities, and the six principal communities have high schools where the children receive Western educations. However, this opportunity presents a mixed blessing. On one hand, Kuna children obtain an education that prepares them to face the world outside of the region; on the other, they learn Spanish and the culture of the white people before they learn our own traditions. They begin to prefer the music of others to our rituals, the attractions of the city to the work of the country. They begin to lose their Kuna identity.

The influence of the Western culture has resulted in the adoption of an attitude of contempt for agricultural work, causing a noticeable decrease in harvests. To confront this influence and continue managing the natural resources in accordance with our traditions, PEMASKY maintains a series of courses and workshops about nature tourism, management of wild-lands, and the training of forest rangers. Its aim is to prepare personnel to ensure that the project always remains in the hands of well-trained Kunas.

The Kunas have always lived in harmony with nature, but some traditional activities, like the rotation of crops and the extraction of food and materials from the forest, make only adequate provisions at best for a small population. Now that we are many, our resource base cannot support the added demands. The general management plan for Kuna Yala addresses this problem, but economic limitations and the lack of sufficient personnel to develop the programs established in the plan have prevented us from putting its recommendations into practice.

Many national and binational organizations, as well as private foundations, have helped us during the first phase of the project, which entailed planning and installing some infrastructure. However, we currently lack the economic support to execute specific programs, such as socioeconomic research to determine the real and present needs of the Kuna people, creation of pilot Kuna-style agroforestry parcels, and implementation of ecotourism. Nor do we have sufficient professional personnel to dedicate to these activities, although we hope to have more professionals soon. Also lacking is the decided support of politicians for our projects that respond to the need for sustainable development.

Our Hope for the Future

Until now we have been able to maintain our political and administrative autonomy, although we have accepted the integration of certain innova-tions that we consider part of cultural development. A typical case is Western education, which we accept, in the words of leader Nele Kantule, as an instrument for the Indian,

> not to brandish it against their noble culture, nor against their healthy customs, but so that their culture will be more fertile, more vigorous, more brilliant, and so that their people will be more respected, more dignified and honorable in the world in which we live.

We have also accepted the concept that our district should be managed as a biosphere reserve, with the technical and financial assistance of national and international organizations. This concept interests us because it emphasizes the need to keep our culture alive and to live in a close relationship with nature. This has always been the mandate of our lead-ers, urging us to conserve and maintain the wildlife to satisfy the needs of future generations.

Our desire is to continue defending our vision of the natural world. However, we will only be able to do this with the support of conserva-tionists who are aware of the Kuna vision of the natural world and are ready to give us unconditional help. We must maintain our autonomy and ensure the survival of the tropical forests, which are our sustenance.

The principal ethics and philosophies of the Kuna and other indigenous people concerning the management and conservation of resources could serve as an example for the rest of the world. An indigenous people who have been able to manage their environment respectfully, combining ancient knowledge with modern techniques to reinforce their harmony with nature, are an example worth following.

For us, the forests are the home of powerful spirits. Each one has its own sacred site, where plants and animals are born. Our tradition says that the spirits hang their clothes from the tops of the highest trees. If we cut down those trees, the spirits will become furious and will punish us.

But the spirits have not been alone in filling us with a respect for nature. Generation after generation, we Kunas have been learning how we depend on the Earth, how one species depends on another, how its death could ultimately effect ours. And so we have learned that, by ensuring the life of Mother Earth, we are ensuring the life of our people.

Notes

1. The Comarca Kuna Yala is the name Kuna Indians give to the Comarca San Blas, a district on the eastern coast of Panamá.

2. "Plan de Manejo para la Comarca de la Biosphera de Kuna Yala" or the "Management Plan for the District of the Kuna Yala Biosphere."

3 | In Honduras

Water for a Thirsty City

Rigoberto Romero Meza
Francisco Martínez Gallegos

On the steep hills of Tegucigalpa, the capital of Honduras, the potable water supply presents a grave problem. The rapidly growing numbers of campesino immigrants, who come seeking education, homes, potable water, and sanitary services and who live in belts of poverty surrounding the city, do not have access to municipal services. Forced to provide for themselves, they buy water of doubtful quality—generally from sources contaminated by industrial chemical waste, soaps, and other domestic pollutants—from street vendors, who transport it in rusty barrels or receptacles that have been used to store pesticides or other toxic substances. The peasants have to pay up to fifty times the official rate for this water, which they then have to carry back through the hilly streets in buckets, sometimes over great distances.

Even the sector of the population that has access to municipal services suffers shortages of water during the dry season. To get through the most critical periods, the privileged classes depend on large capacity storage tanks for their homes.

At the same time, and largely due to the influx of campesinos, the population of the capital is skyrocketing, doubling every 12 years. At this rate, the city will have almost 2 million inhabitants by the year 2010. The demand for potable water in Tegucigalpa, which doubled between 1980 and 1990, will have increased 375 percent by the year 2000 and by 2010 will be almost seven times what it was in 1980.

Unfortunately, the water supplies for Tegucigalpa have already reached their productive limit, and their capacities are decreasing daily with the disappearance of the forests. Worse yet, the rivers that supply the city are contaminated by the frequent applications of agrochemicals such as fungicides, insecticides, and fertilizers—inevitable byproducts of the agricultural systems traditionally used along the course of the river. These problems, coupled with the growing populations along the riverbanks, all increase the process of soil erosion, which in turn causes the concentration of sediments that obstruct reservoirs. Meanwhile, treating the water to make it potable becomes ever more complicated and onerous. As the viable sources of water keep getting farther from the city, requiring large investments in pipes, installations, and connections, the

34

costs of conduction increase.

The National Autonomous Water Service (SANAA), the state institution in charge of administering potable water, supplies water to the 63 percent of the Tegucigalpa population with access to the service. This supply comes principally from five sub-watersheds included in the upper region of the Choluteca watershed. When these sources are insufficient, SANAA resorts to water from subterranean wells. The two most productive sources, however, are La Tigra National Park and the Guacerique River.

The watershed of the Guacerique River clearly shows the deterioration of Tegucigalpa's water sources. In the upper reaches of the river, the forests are constantly being cut, mostly to establish subsistence agriculture, particularly vegetables. These crops use large quantities of agrochemicals that eventually end up in the Guacerique River. In addition, forest fires, extraction of firewood for domestic use, overgrazing, sewage from various military installations, and sedimentation all aggravate the problem by lowering the capacity of the area to produce water of acceptable quantity and quality.

In contrast, La Tigra National Park, a cloud forest situated 11 kilometers (7 miles) northeast of the capital, has an abundance of high-quality water that is collected from about 25 different points. During the winter, La Tigra produces more water (56,160 cubic meters or 14.8 million gallons a day) than all the other sources combined. As a result, La Tigra supplies close to 40 percent of Tegucigalpa's demand for water.

Clearly, of the two most productive sources, La Tigra is the best alternative. In 1985, the treatment costs per cubic meter were 23 times lower for water from La Tigra than for water from the Los Laureles Reservoir in the Guacerique River Basin. The purification of water at the Los Laureles plant requires large quantities of chemicals, most of which are imported at high prices. At La Tigra, on the other hand, the water quality is so high that chemical treatment is minimal. Moreover, the cost of pumping, which for Los Laureles represents 1.5 million lempiras (U.S. $600,000) annually, is not an issue at La Tigra since the water moves by gravity.

If La Tigra were affected by the same problems of deforestation and contamination as Los Laureles, the cost of water production would increase by almost 4 million lempiras (U.S. $1.6 million) per year. Adding to that the cost of pumping, we can say that the savings La Tigra represents amount to more than 5.5 million lempiras (U.S. $2.2 million) per year.

How La Tigra Was Born

Honduras, situated in the central part of the Central American isthmus, is the second largest country in the region, with an expanse of 112,088 square kilometers (43,277 square miles). It has 5.3 million inhabitants, 60 percent of whom work in the agricultural sector.

Photo 3.1 Tegucigalpa Residents Carrying Water: Many residents of Tegucigalpa have to travel long distances over steep hills to fetch water for domestic use. *Credit: IUCN Archives*

Figure 3.1   La Tigra National Park

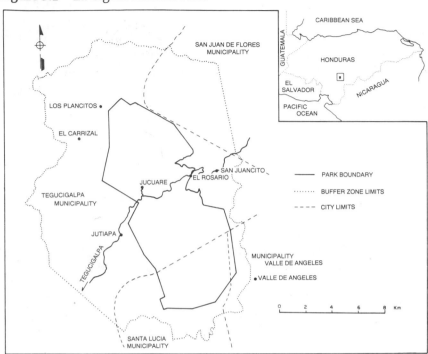

Of the land that should be used only for forestry, more than half has been transformed into cow pastures over the last 20 years. Today, ranching occupies most of the country's agricultural land, even though the income from exportation of coffee and bananas is greater than that from beef.

La Tigra National Park, which took its name from a mountain in the San Juancito Range, is situated in Francisco Morazán Department within the municipalities of Tegucigalpa, Santa Lucía, Valle de Ángeles, and San Juan de Flores (Figure 3.1). Before the Spaniards arrived, this region was inhabited by Chorotega Indians.

During the colonial period, the zone was known and exploited for its mineral riches. Toward the end of the nineteenth century, the Rosario Mining Company of New York set up shop in the region and dedicated itself to extracting gold and silver from the mountains. The company was active in San Juancito for 73 years (1881-1954). Its use of wood for construction of buildings and of infrastructure to process the mineral, as well as for railroad ties and tunnel supports, marked the beginning of the disappearance of the mountain range's forests.

Many of the mine workers settled in various agricultural communities, including San Juancito, Valle de Angeles, Nuevo Rosario, Jutiapa, and Jucuare. When the company ceased its activities, those miners became farmers and turned mainly to the cultivation of flowers, vegetables, and coffee.

At that time, the population of Tegucigalpa got most of its water from La Tigra. However, the frequent use of agrochemicals on the vegetable fields in neighboring settlements was already beginning to threaten the purity of the water. Meanwhile, the local people continued to extract firewood from the forest for domestic use, to hunt there, and to collect ornamental plants to sell in the capital.

In 1952 both the forest and the water supply were so threatened that the government decided to protect an area of some 2,000 hectares (nearly 5,000 acres), which is today the south sector of the park. Accord No. 12 of July 3, 1952, which created this reserve, called for the protection of various rivers that currently supply the city of Tegucigalpa. From that day on, the cutting of trees in the watersheds was prohibited to safeguard the capital's water source. In 1966 the government decided to add almost 23,820 hectares (over 58,800 acres) to the La Tigra Forest Reserve.

In 1977 the first preliminary inventory studies were completed to determine what resources existed in the reserve. Then in 1980 a Decree of Executive Power created La Tigra National Park, finally signaling recognition of the area's ecological, educational, research, and recreational values.

The main goals of the decree include ensuring a supply of water that is constant and of good quality, conserving the forest's biological and cultural riches, and converting La Tigra into a pilot area to serve as an example for other protected areas and their neighboring zones. To these ends, the decree prohibits cutting trees and taking animals and plants from the park; this includes any products or derivatives, as well as any objects of historical or archeological interest.

In addition to defining the park, the decree also defines a buffer zone, the function of which is to reduce the impact of human activities on the protected area. It must be recognized, however, that the boundaries of the park and buffer zone are not defined based on the biophysical characteristics, nor was the social situation of the populations in the area taken into account at that time. By 1988, some 10,000 people lived in the area, according to data taken from that year's census; of those, 9.2 percent lived within the park's borders while the rest lived in the buffer zone.

Objectives of La Tigra National Park

- Preserve the potential of the park, the principal source of water for the capital, the villages, and isolated settlements.
- Conserve remaining forests by maintaining the integrity of the flora and fauna and restoring affected areas, as well as by protecting the natural beauty of the surroundings and the buffer zone.

Photo 3.2 Campesinos Gathering Wood: Severe degradation has taken place in the Guacerique River Basin as a result of deforestation for agriculture and grazing. Forest fires, the gathering of wood for domestic use, overgrazing, and sedimentation all exacerbate the problem. *Credit: IUCN Archives*

- Provide recreational opportunities to the public, concentrating on activities that permit environmental education.

Like a Giant Sponge: The Ecological Park

The protected area of La Tigra National Park is a dense forest that covers 7,600 hectares (18,772 acres, or 29 square miles) of steep hills. There, for each kilometer traveled, one climbs some 150 meters (490 feet); in three-quarters of the park, the slopes can be as steep as 50 to 75 degrees. A mountain climber would have a great time scaling the park's green heights, which rise from 1,000 to 2,300 meters (3,300–7,550 feet). But with all its abrupt ascents, the narrow forest is never more than 15 kilometers (9 miles) wide.

The buffer zone, on the lower slopes of the mountain range, extends over 16,000 hectares (39,520 acres, or 62 square miles), more than double the expanse of the park. Although the greater part of this zone has slopes of more than 30 degrees and some slopes, especially in the south, are as steep as those in the protected area, overall the buffer zone is less irregular than La Tigra.

In both the park and its surroundings, the soils are shallow and of low natural fertility. These white and reddish soils on the steep slopes make the entire region very susceptible to erosion. Agriculture is risky in areas like this.

A cloud forest like the one that covers La Tigra, with high humidity and constant, cold fog, creates ideal conditions for an abundance of orchids, mosses, bromeliads, and other epiphytic plants that live on the trees. Tree ferns, reminiscent of prehistoric times, and entangled vines, like innumerable tentacles that hang from the canopy of the trees, give the forest an atmosphere of dense mystery. Three ecological life zones within La Tigra contribute to the natural richness of the park and ensure a diversity of species to maintain the equilibrium of the ecosystem. All this makes La Tigra a kind of sponge that stores and releases an abundance of crystalline water.

Depending on the life zone and altitude, the dry season lasts between two and five months and the rainy season, between seven and ten. On the mountain slopes where people tend to concentrate, the climate and soil permit the cultivation of basic grains, vegetables, and potatoes. It is possible that some permanent crops and agroforestry systems with species from temperate zones could also be introduced to this region.

Trees found in the park are those typical of highland forests, such as the mountain oak (*Quercus tomentocaulis*), the sweetgum (*Luquidambar styraciflua*), and, above all, the cypress (*Podocarpus oleifolius*). In addition, La Tigra encompasses a multitude of plants with medicinal potential, both curative and preventive. An example of this is *calagüala* (*Polypodium*), a fern that contains active properties capable of curing skin diseases and some types of leukemia. The same is true for prickly ash (*Zanthoxylum foliosum*), and numerous species whose benefits have yet to be explored.

Although a cloud forest does not have as many animals as a rain forest, various species can be found within La Tigra National Park. Many of these are threatened with extinction, both nationally and internationally. To date, three species of amphibians and thirteen species of snakes have been reported; included among the latter are the blind snake (*Typhlops costarricensis*), which is rare, and the coral snake (*Micrurus nigrocinctus*) and the viper (*Bothrops godmani*), which are venomous.

Mammals are abundant. At least thirty-one species are known to live in the park. Of those, six are considered in danger of extinction, two are threatened, and two are considered rare. Standing out in this group are the mountain lion (*Felis concolor*), the margay (*F. weidii*), and the ocelot (*F. pardalis*), as well as the peccary (*Dycotiles tajacu*) and the rare coataquil (*Bassariscus sumichrasti*).

Birds also abound within the park. Of the 171 species that have been identified there, 42 always live in the cloud forest and 27 are migratory, visiting La Tigra during the North American winter. Some of them, such as the resplendent quetzal (*Pharomachrus moccinno*) and the wild turkey (*Crax rubra*), are in danger of extinction.

All these threatened species, and even some living fossils such as the arborescent ferns (*Alsophila salvinii* and *Lophosoria cuadripinnata*), could disappear forever with their habitat—the cloud forest. The protection of these riches will not only help to conserve an important source of products and services for future generations, but will also permit the delivery of water to the present generation.

In the zone neighboring the park, which has been altered by man, the flora is different. There, colonizing species and introduced species abound. In some sections of this zone, one can find young, naturally regenerated forests, which could conveniently be connected to the protected area.

For the People: The Recreational Park

The park has two different access routes. The first is a paved road that runs from Tegucigalpa to Valle de Angeles and then becomes an unpaved road that leads to the village of San Juancito and from there to the camp at Nuevo Rosario; the total trip by this route is 44 kilometers (27 miles). A shorter route (22 kilometers, or 13.6 miles) is the road that leads from Tegucigalpa to Hatillo, continuing to Jutiapa and on to the visitors' center in that sector.

At the moment, the park has neither the infrastructure nor sufficient recreational facilities for visitors. Some trails that traverse the park have existed since the era of mineral exploitation; others have been constructed recently both for vigilance and for use by visitors.

There are two recreational areas in La Tigra. The principal administration post is in Nuevo Rosario, where up to forty visitors can be accommodated in the old hospital of the mining company. The rustic installations include an information center, trails, signs, and a radio communications system. The administrative center in the other recreational area, Jutiapa, has even less infrastructure. This sector scarcely has housing for personnel; it does, however, have a visitors' center, some nature trails with basic information about the forest, an orchid collection with native species as well as species from other areas of the country, and a radio communications system.

Since the basic installations have begun to function and the park's touristic attractions have been promoted, the number of visitors has increased from 1,000 in 1985 to almost 6,500 per year. Although the park is visited year-round, peak seasons are from March to May, when the climate is more agreeable, and from July to September, which coincides with mid-year vacations and national holidays for the schools. According to the registers, 80 percent of the visitors are Hondurans and the rest are foreign tourists.

Guardians of La Tigra

Although the principal responsibility for La Tigra National Park lies with the Secretariat of Natural Resources, help for projects comes from other institutions as well. Such is the case of SANAA, which manages all aspects related to water, and the Honduran Corporation for Forestry Development (COHDEFOR), which directs actions for protection of forests.

The nongovernmental organization World Neighbors has done important work in the southeast sector of the park. It is currently directing a program for sustainable agriculture based on nontraditional models of production that do not use agrochemicals and do not depend on external inputs. These production models actively promote conservation and soil improvement.

Since 1984, the Honduras Association for Ecology (AHE), another nongovernmental organization, has been participating in the protection and management of the park. Its work has included looking for international funding to finance the administration of the park and many of its activities.

Among the organizations that have worked with AHE, the World Wildlife Fund (WWF) stands out for its constant collaboration, both in contracting and training personnel for environmental education and in financing the purchase of field equipment and the construction of buildings, especially for the public use and operations programs. WWF has also cooperated with outreach work in the communities, seeking solutions to the inevitable conflicts that arise when the necessities of production in a community clash with the need for potable water for the citizens of the capital.

Other international conservation organizations, such as the World Conservation Union (IUCN), the Tropical Agricultural Center for Research and Education (CATIE), and the Wild Wings Foundations of the United States, have contributed their technical and financial support. And bilateral aid organizations such as the U.S. Agency for International Development (USAID), the Inter-American Foundation of the United States (IAF), and the Canadian International Development Agency (CIDA) have also given support.

Providing for the Future

In 1986 the difficulty of obtaining potable water for Tegucigalpa was so critical that a seminar/workshop was organized for decision-making personnel in institutions that were, in one way or other, involved in the problem. The seminar, entitled "Potable Water for Tegucigalpa: Who Is Responsible?" was run under the auspices of AHE, CATIE, IUCN, and the Secretariat for Planning, Coordination, and Budget (SECPLAN).

One of the most important conclusions of the workshop was that the park's importance as a source of water for the capital necessitated its protection from the growing threat posed by the demand for agricultural land in the area. Such protection would entail working with the populations neighboring the park, promoting alternative agricultural technologies and offering recreational and environmental programs. To meet this need, AHE and IUCN, with financing from CIDA, formulated the project "Development of La Tigra National Park and Its Buffer Zone" in 1987.

The consulting team that prepared the project also prepared a proposal to finance it, which is being studied by the Honduran government and CIDA. A few months earlier, that same team had prepared an operative plan for the park with support from WWF and CATIE. This plan contains a program of ecodevelopment that includes aspects of conservation as well as rational use of the land bordering the park.

The park development project focuses its attention on land use planning and watershed management. It also considers conservation and agrochemical use, as well as legal and institutional matters. One important problem, however, involves what the creation of the park has cost the park's neighbors in terms of restrictions in land use, land tenancy, use of wildlife, and extraction of wood for firewood and construction. Although the project proposes ways to ameliorate these difficulties, these measures are not yet being implemented.

To protect and administrate the national park, some efforts are already under way in both the protected area and in the neighboring zone. In the

Photo 3.3 Cattle Grazing Near Park Border: The park limits some of the activities of the neighboring communities, such as wood cutting, farming, grazing and land ownership. However, the management project does propose measures to counteract these limitations. *Credit: Oscar Lucke*

park, activities center on five principal areas: training of personnel, infrastructure, environmental education, research, and planning.

Considering the need to work with and for the region's inhabitants, such aspects as promotion, training, and development of human resources are of the highest importance. The scarcity of personnel trained to manage and develop protected areas limits effective work and prevents the maximum use of existing resources. Thus, training concentrates on technical instruction for the personnel of public and private institutions involved in park management. Given the characteristics of the nuclear family and the role the mother plays in the use of natural resources, the training, organization, and promotion of women in the communities are also included.

Another priority area is the construction and maintenance of buildings and basic services for the park's personnel and visitors. As noted previously, the park's current infrastructure includes a visitors' center, educational center, and housing for personnel.

Environmental education in both the park and the neighboring zone focuses on activities with elementary school teachers from the neighboring areas, training events for groups from local communities, workshops about appropriate technologies and soil conservation, study tours, and the production of some educational materials to support these activities. Work is also being done in the areas of environmental interpretation, public relations, and broadcasting. Education is directed as much at visitors and neighbors of the park as it is at politicians, administrators, and inhabitants of the capital. This work should be intensified and extended to other groups in the future.

In the area of research, various institutions are taking advantage of La Tigra's potential to complete inventories of flora and fauna, periodically check water quality, and conduct field trips and graduate research.

Though the management plan calls for work in the buffer zone, as of yet this work has barely begun; we are still seeking financing for many of its components. Nevertheless, studies and research projects in the buffer zone are establishing an inventory to serve as the basis for future actions. For work in the area of socioeconomic development, we hope to collaborate with the inhabitants of the zone in agricultural, animal husbandry, and agroforestry activities.

Lastly, the sale of tourist services could, in the near future, also benefit the inhabitants of the area and help finance the management of the park.

Unfortunately, one of the main difficulties in managing La Tigra is the diversity of institutions and organizations—currently, twenty governmental and eighteen nongovernmental—with some type of responsibility for the park. The functions and responsibilities of each are so unclear that it is common to find two institutions doing the same thing. The prevailing lack of coordination results in a constant waste of time and resources. To combat this problem, the project for managing the reserve intends to establish mechanisms of coordination between all the institutions that work there. It also recommends revising the legislation related to managing the protected areas.

The essential role that La Tigra National Park plays in supplying potable water for the inhabitants of the capital underscores the need to protect this important biological site. In this regard, the efforts of neighboring populations to maintain the water quality and conserve the park and its diversity are indispensable and should be supported through environmental education and training in the use of nontraditional agricultural methods. Such tools will not only improve their incomes but also help to convert the park's neighboring populations into its protectors.

Thus it is hoped that, in 1991, the government of Honduras and the CIDA will approve a proposal for financing management of La Tigra and its area of influence. If this happens, La Tigra could continue supplying its clean waters to the capital, and perhaps one day the inhabitants of Tegucigalpa, instead of crossing the steep hills of the city carrying buckets of contaminated water, can have in their homes the same crystal water they enjoy while hiking up the verdant trails of that lovely cloud forest.

4 | Ecotourism Costa Rican Style

Tamara Budowski

Tourism brochures describe the Costa Rica of the 1990s as a paradise of nature and tranquillity. They invite tourists to awaken to the roar of the howler monkeys and enjoy typical meals and adventures while learning about the exuberance of the natural world.

It was not always like this. A few years ago, our country tried to attract tourists by inviting them to get to know a "country of peace" and suggesting, "We have so much to share." Today our nation attracts visitors who want to discover, study, and enjoy our natural areas, the beauty of our landscapes, and the diverse species of plants and animals that inhabit so small a territory. Entrepreneurs from different nations visit us in search of ideas about how to develop this "ecological" tourism in their own countries; photographers, journalists, writers, and researchers also come to study and document this phenomenon.

At the same time, a two-and-a-half-year program for a master's degree in ecotourism was recently established in our country, and Costa Ricans travel throughout the world to assess and consult on this trend in other countries. The international media, which earlier had never even heard of the term *ecotourism*, have lately begun to cover the theme with more frequency; they say the word is "hot" because of its great popularity and the interest it has awakened. And in their coverage, Costa Rica is often referred to as a model country in the development of ecotourism.[1]

Perhaps the best way to understand this phenomenon is through a description offered by Héctor Ceballos-Lascurain, a consultant for the World Conservation Union, in 1988:

> Ecotourism . . . implies a relocation to zones that are relatively little altered and contaminated, with the specific purpose of studying, admiring, and enjoying the scenic beauty, the flora and fauna, and existing cultural aspects (past and present) found in the areas. Ecological tourism implies a scientific, aesthetic, or philosophical appreciation, without the ecological tourist necessarily being a scientist, artist, or professional philosopher. A principal point is that the person who practices ecotourism has the opportunity to enter into contact with nature, in a very different form than they experience in their urban or routine lives. This person will eventually develop a consciousness that will convert him/her into a person sincerely involved in aspects related to the conservation of nature.

Karen Ziffer, in a recent paper entitled "Ecotourism: The Uneasy Alliance,"[2] writes that ecotourism is "a movement that potentially involves billions of dollars, high-level politics, the survival of threatened cultures, and the preservation of natural zones that are rapidly disappearing."

But where does this growing interest in ecotourism come from? To begin with, the tourist industry in general has the highest growth index in the world. Today it is the third largest generator of foreign exchange, and by the year 2000 tourism is estimated to become the principal source of revenues on our planet. This growth is seen as much in traditional tourism, which concentrates on developed areas where conventional activities are offered, as in specialized tourism, which is found in less developed areas and consists of the search for unique activities that are more directly a function of the particular environment and culture. At the same time, the global awareness that has focused on conservation of the environment has added an ecological dimension to the tourism industry as such themes as global warming, destruction of the ozone layer, disappearance of tropical jungles, and environmental contamination have awakened in people a desire to appreciate nature and to fight for its survival.

From another perspective, the appeal of this trend can be traced back to the search for profound and enriching experiences that characterized the decade of the sixties. Just as this search resulted in the popularity of outdoor activities in the seventies, the awakened preoccupation with health, natural foods, and good physical condition in the eighties led directly to the development of ecotourism, which is attracting more people every day.

There are few places in the world that have yet to be developed or explored. In Costa Rica, ecotourism is concentrated in those wild zones in which exploration has been minimal. These include private reserves such as Monteverde and La Selva, which are managed by not-for-profit institutions, and Marenco, Tiskita, Rara Avis, Magil, Selva Verde, Talahari, and El Gavilán, which are managed by tourist companies. Ecotourism also thrives in natural areas of great scenic beauty, especially the national parks (Figure 4.1). The tourist of the nineties can be profiled as a person who wants to get to know the few natural zones that still survive and who seeks uncommon activities that offer new intellectual and spiritual experiences.

With an expanse of approximately 51,000 square kilometers (19,575 square miles), Costa Rica has more than a half-million hectares (over 1,930 square miles) of protected areas within the system of parks and reserves. These areas are divided into 34 units that comprise coral reefs on both coasts; wet zones like mangrove swamps, rain forests, tropical dry forests, and even cloud forests; volcanoes; and tropical paramo (high barren land). The National Park Service also protects caverns and historical and archeological sites, as well as beaches that are preserved as much for their ecological importance (various species of marine turtles arrive at

Figure 4.1   National Parks of Costa Rica

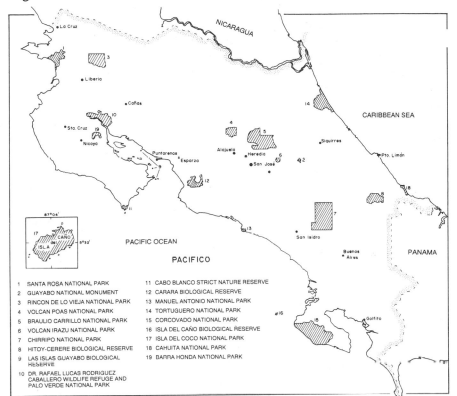

1   SANTA ROSA NATIONAL PARK
2   GUAYABO NATIONAL MONUMENT
3   RINCON DE LO VIEJA NATIONAL PARK
4   VOLCAN POAS NATIONAL PARK
5   BRAULIO CARRILLO NATIONAL PARK
6   VOLCAN IRAZU NATIONAL PARK
7   CHIRRIPO NATIONAL PARK
8   HITOY-CERERE BIOLOGICAL RESERVE
9   LAS ISLAS GUAYABO BIOLOGICAL RESERVE
10 DR. RAFAEL LUCAS RODRIGUEZ CABALLERO WILDLIFE REFUGE AND PALO VERDE NATIONAL PARK
11 CABO BLANCO STRICT NATURE RESERVE
12 CARARA BIOLOGICAL RESERVE
13 MANUEL ANTONIO NATIONAL PARK
14 TORTUGUERO NATIONAL PARK
15 CORCOVADO NATIONAL PARK
16 ISLA DEL CAÑO BIOLOGICAL RESERVE
17 ISLA DEL COCO NATIONAL PARK
18 CAHUITA NATIONAL PARK
19 BARRA HONDA NATIONAL PARK

them annually to lay their eggs) as for their scenic beauty. It is notable that the great majority of the forests remaining in Costa Rica are in protected zones; the rest have been devasted or are being gradually destroyed.

The easy access to these protected zones and their proximity to one another permit tourists to visit various parks and reserves during a short stay in the country. In addition, there are more than forty hotels, hostels, and lodges near the national parks and private reserves, and more than twenty guides who specialize in ecotourism are available to offer visitors assistance and information.

The Growth of Ecotourism in Costa Rica

Ecotourism began in the last century when important scientists, attracted by Costa Rica's political stability and biological diversity, came to study our flora and fauna. Because their work prompted the arrival of more researchers, these scientists became the first promoters of ecotourism. Visits of this nature then increased significantly in the early 1960s, mostly due to the establishment in our country of the Organization for Tropical Studies (OTS). Through the years, this institution has dedicated itself to attracting students, researchers, and professors, who come to study about and teach courses on Costa Rican plants and wildlife.

Through their numerous publications, these scientists have made Costa Rica and its great biodiversity known. Many of them have given us the material our guides now use to explain the biological processes to tourists; additionally, their scientific research has provided our national scientists with the foundation needed to plan the creation of new national parks. Without the knowledge and conclusions generated by the scientists, both national and foreign, and especially by the biologists among them, we would not have as many areas under protection. Nor would we have that valuable information that permits us to better understand Costa Rican nature and make public the need to protect it. It is important to emphasize here the key role those researchers have played in forming the basis for ecotourism; ecotourism could not exist without the previously documented knowledge of the natural phenomena that are studied and seen during the tours.

In the early 1980s, a new wave of tourism began flowing toward the wild zones as the scientists were joined by nature lovers who came to spend their vacations in our national parks. But this new wave did not initially enjoy government support. Rather, it was private enterprise (hotels, lodges, travel agencies) that got behind it, both nationally and internationally, using advertising and such public relations tools as promotional trips to attract attention to Costa Rica's natural riches. Notable in this effort was the campaign developed by the national airline, LACSA. The company has published numerous folders on the theme and has dedicated a significant amount of space in its magazine, *LACSA's World*, to articles related to Costa Rican nature. Then in 1985, the Costa Rican Institute of Tourism (ICT) lent its support to the new tourist current through its promotional campaigns that emphasized the beauty of the country with the slogan "Costa Rica is . . . natural." All this material projected to millions of potential tourists the image of a country of extreme natural beauty and a wealth of flora and fauna.

In a survey conducted by the ICT during the peak season of 1986, nearly 75 percent of those interviewed said that "the principal reason that [they] chose Costa Rica as a tourist destination" was its natural beauty, and 36 percent said they came specifically to observe Costa Rica's nature. From this second statistic, we can conclude that more than one-third of the peak-season visitors that year were ecotourists. Two years later, one of every two tourists interviewed during peak season reported having visited a natural site such as a national park, biological reserve, forest reserve, or wildlife refuge. Similarly, visits to seven of the major national parks increased 50 percent between 1986 and 1988, with the number of foreign visitors growing twice as fast as that of national visitors. Perhaps even more telling is the fact that tourism in 1988 generated about $170 million in our country, 13 percent of the total money earned by Costa Rican exports.

In 1987 Dr. Oscar Arias Sanchez, then president of Costa Rica, received the Nobel Peace Prize. This, together with his government's strong conservation policies, undoubtedly helped attract much world attention to our country during the years that followed and was largely responsible for the increase in ecotourism. Fortunately, in the short time since Raphael Angel Calderón Fournier took office in May 1990, his administration has revealed a profound interest in continuing Arias's conservation policies. Support for the development of ecotourism is also evident, inspiring hope of a promising future for Costa Rica in this area.

The Ecotourists of the Nineties

There are many tourists who, attracted by an interest in natural history and the beauty of our nature, have grown bored with traditional destinations and artificial activities and seek a different experience. These people, most of whom are college educated, want to explore and share the customs and culture of the visited country. Although their incomes vary, most—with the possible exception of students, professors, and researchers—come from the highest socioeconomic classes. And most fall into two large and well-defined age groups: baby boomers, people born during the demographic explosion that occurred between 1946 and 1964; and senior citizens—retired people or those older than 65 years, including the "empty nest" couples, whose children have left home.

North Americans have an interesting terminology that allows us to further classify the baby boomers into "Yuppies" (Young Upwardly Mobile Professionals), young professionals aged 26–35 who are climbing the socioeconomic ladder; and "Dinks" (Double Income, No Kids), couples aged 35–45 who do not have children and who both work and bring home income. These two groups find it unacceptable to spend a few days lying on the beach as people their age did a few years ago. Instead, they want their vacations to offer a challenge, however small it may be, and they want to return home in better physical condition, having had some original experience.

Added to these is a new class of ecotourists that has recently begun to appear: baby boomers with children, who have no desire to return to traditional tourism but would rather travel with their children to where they can come in contact with nature and become familiar with new cultures without taking too many risks. For these people, Costa Rica offers a privileged situation because it has facilities appropriate for children. These include easy trails, comfortable hotels, health centers close to the natural areas, and relatively good conditions of hygiene that meet

Photo 4.1 Glacial Lake: The natural beauty of Costa Rica, combined with a well developed park system, has contributed to the growth of ecotourism. The country's diverse landscape includes volcanoes, coral reefs, highland plains, and mangroves. *Credit: Mayra Bonilla*

international standards. Some tours have already been developed with various families and have been very successful. And every day more and more families are visiting the natural zones of our country on their own.

Ecotourists can also be classified according to other factors, such as the degree of physical challenge they seek or the depth to which they want to study a specific aspect of nature. Thus, we can identify two relatively distinct groups:

1. *Scientific tourists*: scientists and students who travel for educational or research reasons and who therefore generally remain here for longer periods of time, make use of regular services (family restaurants and public transportation), and stay in moderately priced hotels.

2. *Nature tourists*: people whose passion for nature is personal rather than professional. These nature lovers fall into three groups:

   a. The hard-nature tourists—bird-watchers, horticulturists, orchid lovers, and so forth—are interested in a specific aspect of nature, and their trip revolves around that theme. These people are generally willing to tolerate rigorous conditions such as early hours, less sophisticated food and accommodations, and other discomforts as long as they can satisfy the expectations of their visit.

   b. The soft-nature tourists, on the other hand, are interested in various natural attractions, and they travel to observe the nature, wildlife, and culture of an area without particular emphasis. These tourists—the fastest growing segment both internationally and in Costa Rica—include those who travel more for "fashion" than from a genuine interest in nature, and who have the lowest level of knowledge about and preparation for the facilities and sites to be visited. As such, they require a higher level of services and accommodations, seek more relaxing activities, and are less tolerant of discomforts, such as a bath without hot water, than the previous group.

   c. Finally, the adventure tourists are those who are less interested in understanding the interrelations of the diverse organisms in our forests than in enjoying the outdoors and using both protected and unprotected zones. Their stay is linked to the practice of some sport, such as fishing, hiking, horseback riding, bicycling, surfing, skin diving, or white-water river rafting. Whether these tourists can rightly be considered ecotourists is debatable, given that surfing, for example, is actually more a function of a particular type of wave than of the natural riches of a country and fishing "consumes" part of the natural resource, which detracts somewhat from the philosophy of "observation without destruction." Still, fishing has also been influenced by conservationist ideas; every day more fishermen are releasing their fish after having experienced the thrill of catching them. And every day, more adventure tourists are becoming interested in learning about the natural history and environmental problems of areas visited.

Of these two groups, nature tourism is the segment of specialized tourism that generates the most visitors to the wild areas of Costa Rica. By the mid-1980s, it was considered to be the segment of the U. S. tourism industry with the greatest growth, contributing between 5 and 10 percent of the $27.5 billion spent by North Americans on tourism in 1985. In 1986 the United States already had about 5,000 operators, guide services, and travel agencies specializing in this branch (*Wall Street Journal*, June 30, 1986). Recent data reported by various North American companies indicate an annual growth rate in sales of nature tourism on the order of 20 percent.

A Mixed Blessing

The Benefits of Ecotourism

Ecotourism is a type of tourism that is more educated and respectful of the host culture. Practiced by what is today called a responsible tourist— one who comes to learn about and become familiar with the culture and environment of the destination—it generally has a positive impact on the location that has attracted it.

In Costa Rica, many small business people earn a living from ecotourism, including boat owners, farmers who rent out horses and provide other services for visitors, and local tourist agents. Ecotourism does not require multimillion-dollar investments as do other types of tourist developments, such as mountain and beach resorts. Facilities for ecotourism, though hospitable and comfortable, tend to be small and rustic and thus require a much lower investment than do facilities for traditional tourism. Moreover, unlike the modern hotels, they respect the local architectural styles and decors, using designs and materials that harmonize with the surrounding environment. At the same time, ecotourism provides money for conservation because many tourists who visit Costa Rica make donations that permit improvement of park services and the purchase of new lands for protection.

Ecotourism has also forced some entrepreneurs to recognize the extent to which their businesses directly depend on the natural resources near their property. Some of these business people have stopped cutting down their forests in order to attract tourists; others have purchased bordering lands to increase their virgin forest holdings—the primary attraction of their installations. Such is the case of the Marenco Biological Station,

Photo 4.2 Ecotourist: Ecotourism does not require multimillion dollar investments. Small local business and entrepreneurs could meet the demands of ecotourists for comfortable lodging, simple meals, and adequate transportation.
Credit: Mayra Bonilla

located near Corcovado National Park; of Rara Avis, which borders both
Braulio Carrillo National Park and the La Selva Protected Zone; and of
the Magil Lodge in Upala. These entrepreneurs also participate in research and conservation projects on both their own and surrounding
properties.

Just as there are entrepreneurs who are promoting the conservation of
the areas near their establishments, so too are entire communities doing
the same thing through volunteer work. In Monteverde, money earned by
guiding people through the reserve, giving talks to tourists, presenting
audiovisuals, and other activities is deposited in a common fund, which
is later used to buy land and increase the area of the reserve.

But above all, ecotourism provides environmental education. By enjoying our protected zones and admiring their beauty, international visitors come to understand the need to preserve them as well as the wild
areas in their own countries. And on seeing so many people coming from
far away to see their natural wonders, Costa Ricans have themselves
grown more appreciative of these treasures and have become their faith-
ful guardians, admirers, and promoters.

The Dangers of Ecotourism Unplanned and Unchecked

Of course, despite all its benefits, ecotourism is not without its drawbacks. Although it has been defined as "travel to natural areas without
damaging or contaminating the wildlife and landscape," in practice this
has not always been the case. In Hawaii, for example, the intensive use of
coastal waters for aquatic sports and the resultant noise from motorboats
have upset the breeding of whales; mother whales and their calves have
had to seek less hospitable areas, thus endangering their survival. In Peru
and Nepal, mountain trails used by tourists have become littered with
garbage. And a 1987 article in the magazine *Destinations* encouraged future visitors to Kenya to hurry, warning that if they waited they would
"find wild areas devastated and overpopulated by tourists"; more than a
million visitors were expected in Kenya in 1990.

Nor has Costa Rica been exempt from such negative consequences.
Camping has been prohibited in Manuel Antonio National Park because
of the pollution it was producing. In Tortugero National Park, where
more hotels are being constructed all the time, you can see more than a
hundred people on the beach at night during sea turtle nesting season.
And tourism in the Monteverde Reserve has caused the deterioration of
trails and surrounding vegetation; birds and animals that were once easy
to see now migrate deeper into the forest. Officials are considering limiting the number of visitors to the reserve to 100 people per day beginning
in 1991. Unfortunately, the region's hotel capacity is 290 people. Thus,
apart from local business people, among those hurt will be the additional
190 ecotourists, who, after traveling so far, will not be permitted to enter

and explore the reserve—their primary reason for visiting.

The situation in Monteverde clearly shows the effects of a lack of planning between the tourism industry and conservation authorities. Another relevant example involves the proposed construction of a dam on the Pacuare River. This dam would eliminate all possibilities of whitewater rafting on that river, which draws thousands of tourists every year. As a result, for the first time we are experiencing a conflict between development and ecotourism in Costa Rica. Much of this conflict is because the institution promoting the project—the Costa Rican Institute of Electricity (ICE)—has completed neither environmental nor social impact studies for the project.

Coming to Terms with Ecotourism

Unfortunately, the government has neither set limitations for certain areas nor promoted new sites of interest for ecotourism. Nor have the authorities planned future touristic developments to be compatible with ecotourism. Instead, in their plans to attract investors, they speak of large-scale projects with thousands of rooms—projects that could damage the natural attractions that draw the ecotourists and thus are completely antagonistic to the philosophy of ecotourism.

Policies are also lacking for training specialized guides. With the growing demand for such services, the number of trained guides who are available to fill that demand is clearly insufficient. The same can be said for the existing interpretive material—pamphlets and books on ecotourism, maps of trails in the parks and reserves, and so on—that is used to explain the natural processes and basic biology to the tourist. Yet these guides and materials are basic elements of ecotourism.

The tourism industry has been similarly remiss in not developing differential pricing policies that would permit it to lower prices during the off (rainy) season and would favor national tourism with lower rates. Such policies would have the advantage of promoting tourism to markets with less buying power—especially Costa Ricans who do not have the economic means that international tourists have.

Finally, even though a large percentage of Costa Rican territory consists of officially declared conservation areas, in practice these sites do not receive all the protection offered them by law. The few personnel who attend them are poorly distributed and inadequately trained to meet the necessities of guarding the areas. Nor are there official guidelines for resolving conflicts of interest, such as those involving the presence of miners, loggers, and settlers within the parks and reserves.

Obviously, without adequate planning, an excess of visitors can damage a region's natural environment, which is the main attraction for the ecotourist. Moreover, ecotourism is based on a close relationship with nature and a sense of solitude that cannot be obtained if there are too many people in the same place. Thus, a cooperative planning effort must be promoted that integrates the needs and concerns of the government, the national and international conservation associations, the tourism promoters, and the tourists themselves.

In keeping with such an effort, immediate measures should be taken to permit parks and reserves to establish not only carrying capacities to regulate the flow of tourists, but also zones for different uses within protected areas, thereby segregating those that are most fragile. This does not mean limiting visits to a park; rather, it calls for arranging various routes of access, trails, and facilities so that the number of visitors can be increased without damage to the area. Consideration should also be given to developing other protected zones that have not been opened to tourists, such as La Amistad National Park, Caño Negro, and Hitoy Cerere. Furthermore, guides should be given the necessary and continually updated training that allows them to practice their profession more efficiently.

In addition, more favorable policies and financing are needed to enable small Costa Rican investors to participate in ecotourism-related activities. Both the U.S. Agency for International Development (USAID) and the Inter-American Development Bank (IDB) have funds available for ecotourism, but the paperwork for obtaining them is so complex and the interest rates so unattractive that in 1989, neither agency funded a single project related to ecotourism. As a result, most investors have been foreigners.

But new investors will not be willing to risk capital on ecotourism if they cannot be assured that the forest that exists today will still be there in 5, 10, or 20 years. Therefore, the tourism industry also has to become more actively involved, first in making business owners realize how vital the natural resources are to their businesses, and then in obtaining and making donations for the conservation of those resources.

When potential investors are identified, consultants are needed to teach them to respect the resources and to develop projects without damaging the natural area. Consultation with and education of communities near the wild zones also should be undertaken to help those communities organize themselves so that they can reap the benefits that ecotourism can bring to their citizens.

Finally, we must guard against our own tendency to oversell. When speaking about some of our national parks, we tend to promote species that are difficult to see, such as jaguars, tapirs, and other species threatened by extinction. But Costa Rica is not Kenya, Tanzania, or Galapagos, where it is easy to see wild animals. Rather than disappoint the tourist by creating expectations that cannot be met, our tourist brochures must instead emphasize that the main attraction of our forests lies as much in the complexity and fragility of our ecosystems as in their natural beauty.

Photo 4.3 Costa Rican "Causel": Despite the variety of wildlife found in Costa Rica, it is generally difficult to see many of these animals in the dense forests. Enthusiastic advertisements to the contrary often raise visitors' expectations, and as a result, many are disappointed. *Credit: Mayra Bonilla*

The Challenge Before Us

Tourism in general contributes to peace by providing socioeconomic benefits that promote the stability of a country and the well-being of its citizens. Since ecotourism is based on the philosophy of respecting life in all its manifestations, it contributes to peace by promoting understanding and friendship between peoples. Conversely, without peace and political stability, a country has little opportunity to profit from the benefits of tourism.

Much can be said about ecotourism, which represents not only one of the most agreeable forms of environmental education but also an excellent economic tool that maintains the equilibrium between use and preservation of a country's natural resources at the same time that it contributes to sustainable development. Nevertheless, we must study this phenomenon more to be able to better understand it, promote it, and avoid potential negative consequences.

Costa Rica has a great responsibility in the world today, standing out as a model on the global level of how to develop a tourism based on nature without damaging the resources that support it. But this model runs grave risks if the development of ecotourism goes unregulated. To the extent that we can correct the errors and prevent the problems that have threatened our success, we will be setting an example for other countries to follow in their efforts to protect their wild areas while supporting themselves with tourism. If we succeed, we will be demonstrating to the world that tourism and conservation can coexist and continue hand in hand into the twenty-first century.

Notes

1. See, for example: "Planet of the Year," *Time*, January 2, 1989, pp. 16–19; "Ecotourism: Where Capitalism and Conservation Meet," *Mexico Journal*, May 22, 1989, p. 18; "World Starting to Take Notice of Costa Rica," *International Herald Tribune*, October 2, 1989, p. 28.

2. Karen Ziffer, "Ecotourism: The Uneasy Alliance," Conservation International Series of Working Papers on Ecotourism, Fall 1989.

5 | A Tomorrow of Forests and Bread

The Case of Nicaragua

Lorenzo Cardenal

In the foothills of the Casita Volcano, in northwestern Nicaragua, a few campesino women work in small nurseries, transplanting saplings from germination trays to plastic bags. These saplings will later be planted in the mountains in an attempt to reestablish the dry forest that has practically disappeared from the area. Meanwhile, when the men are not working their own farms or the land of their cooperatives, they are constructing dikes and planting windbreaks.

Until a few years ago, these campesinos did not dream it possible to one day regreen the mountains that have been bald since the 1950s, victims of a desperate search for farmland and firewood. At that time, the fertile North Pacific plains at the foot of the mountains were invaded by cotton barons; the cultivation of cotton led to the destruction of the remaining dry forest and drove the inhabitants of the zone out toward both the dry, rugged lands of the Central Mountainous Zone and the wet, nutrient-deficient lands of the Caribbean Slope. Much of the rural population migrated to the country's more important cities, especially the capital city of Managua, thus aggravating its problems of overpopulation.

Over the next few decades, Nicaragua suffered the most intense deterioration of its natural resources in its history. By 1980, deforestation had reached a rate of more than 100,000 hectares (385 square miles) per year, one of the highest rates in Central America. The resultant soil erosion, which affected the entire country, amounted to 44 tons of soil per hectare being lost annually. Water began to grow scarce in the area's principal cities. Hardly a river remained that was not contaminated by sewage and pesticide residues. In fact, insecticide pollution on the western side of the country, where the cotton plantations are found, reached such alarming levels that today it is used as a case study in pesticide abuse and the poisoning of farm workers. The toxic concentrations in mothers' milk here is 12 times that of the world average.

Aware of these problems, the Sandinista government, which took power in 1979, created the Nicaraguan Institute of Natural Resources and the Environment (IRENA), the institution responsible for ensuring the rational use of natural resources. IRENA's mandate includes the preparation and implementation of projects for environmental restoration in Nicaragua.

63

Figure 5.1   Veracruz Heroes and Martyrs Project

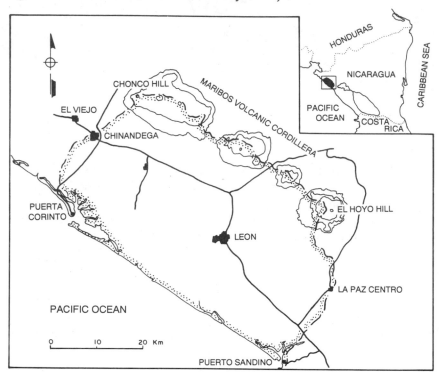

A few months after beginning work, IRENA completed studies that confirmed that the area most affected by the environmental crisis was the western region, especially the area around La Paz Centro, León, and Chinandega (Figure 5.1). To solve that region's most serious problems, the Western Erosion Management Project (PCEO) was created. Based on studies it completed to determine how much soil was being lost to wind and rain, PCEO concluded that forestry plantations, windbreaks, and dikes were needed to stabilize the soils.

By the end of 1985, 1,500 hectares (5.78 square miles) of compact forests had been planted, as well as 1,200 kilometers (744 miles) of windbreaks. Some 4,200 dikes were also constructed to control flash floods, and two small experimental stations were set up to study erosion. These actions not only reduced the agricultural losses of local farmers but also slowed the process of soil erosion.

From this first experience, IRENA established the need to plan land use and restore degraded soils on a wider scale. Thus, the Heroes and Martyrs of Veracruz project was born in 1985, focusing on the most critical areas in the countryside, those around the cities of La Paz Centro and Chinandega.

The Heroes and Martyrs of Veracruz Project

The project covers an area of approximately 2,000 square kilometers (770 square miles) and is located in the extreme south of the León-Chinandega region. Within this area are various watersheds, into which northern waters flow down from the crests of the Maribios volcanic range, pouring southward to the coast and the Pacific Ocean. The project extends west to the heights of Chonco Hill (Cerro del Chonco), south past Chinandega to the port of Corinto, and east to the top of Hoyo Hill (Cerro El Hoyo), comprising La Paz Centro and even reaching Puerto Sandino (Figure 5.1).

The entire project zone is highly populated, reaching a density of almost 190 inhabitants per square kilometer (490 inhabitants per square mile). Of its 376,000 inhabitants, 45 percent live in the country. The rest are concentrated in the cities, especially León, whose history and culture make it Nicaragua's second most important city, and Chinandega, an important agro-industrial center near which is located the San Antonio Sugar Refinery, one of the most important in the country and in Central America.

In the extreme west lies the port of Corinto, from which the country's principal exports are shipped. Because the entire zone is interconnected by an extensive network of roads and railways, Corinto is linked to Nicaragua's most important production centers; this facilitates the shipment of products not just of the zone but of the entire country.

A Land in Peril

The zone marked for recuperation by the Heroes and Martyrs of Veracruz project contains extensive plains with highly fertile volcanic soil. Because this region is dry during the summer, its uncovered expanses face violent winds that carry this rich soil thousands of miles from its place of origin, to be lost forever. During the winter, the same areas succumb to torrential rains, which convert insignificant ditches into turbulent streams; these streams then overflow to sweep across the plains, dislodging tons of topsoil and washing it into the sea. This kind of erosion, which at one time was unknown in the region, has decreased the productive capacity of the soil and, with it, the volume of harvests.

Despite the dryness of the area during summer, there are rich and accessible deposits of water underground. These deposits store more than 130 million cubic meters (34.3 trillion gallons) of water, with which about 50,000 hectares (190 square miles) can be irrigated each year. In addition, since this soil can be easily farmed using extensive and mechanized agricultural systems, some 80,000 hectares (310 square miles)—10 percent of the country's cultivated land—are found in the project zone. Over the last four decades, this land has become Nicaragua's cotton production center. It has also been used for the cultivation of other commercial crops such as

Photo 5.1 Nicaraguan Women Working in a Tree Nursery: At the foot of the Casita Volcano in northeastern Nicaragua, small farmers work enthusiastically on a project to rehabilitate the degraded land. *Credit: Gabriel Travisano*

sugar cane and bananas.

Leaving the plains and moving into the foothills and higher reaches of the mountain range, the land becomes more appropriate for forestry. On this land, wood for fuel and construction could be produced. The land could also serve for the maintenance of wild species like deer and paca, which have long been the preferred target of local hunters. Instead, however, the displacement of the small farmers to these highlands has led to the introduction of agricultural production systems that are inappropriate for that terrain. Thus, the hills that once flowered with luxuriant forest species, which lost their leaves each summer and rebloomed with the rains, are today almost completely desolate.

The intense deforestation of the foothills and the crests of the volcanoes has altered the original pattern of rain runoff. Enormous volumes of water now flow down to the plains in a short period of time, accelerating the process of erosion. The rains and landslides are so heavy that in 1982, they destroyed nearly all the bridges in the region, almost completely paralyzing the area. Close to $20 million had to be invested to get the transportation network functioning again, and even today, the railways have not yet been completely repaired. The destruction also affected crops and homes and took many lives.

Cotton expansion on the plains also displaced campesinos to the coast, where extensive mangrove (*Rhizophora mangle*) swamps serve as hatcheries for lobsters, shrimp, crabs, mussels, and marine fish. The fishermen appreciate the importance of the mangrove swamps, which provide 10,000 hectares (38.59 square miles) of potential use for fishing and firewood harvesting. Yet their value is not solely recreational; most commercial species of fish pass the first part of their lives feeding in and seeking protection among the tortuous mangrove roots that weave through the swamp's waters. In addition, these wetlands provide sanctuary for thousands of birds, such as herons and egrets (*Ardeidae*), pelicans (*Pelecanidae*), and kingfishers (*Alcedinidae*). Lastly, the mangroves form effective barriers that protect the coast from erosion and flooding. Unfortunately, all these valuable resources are threatened by the accumulation of sediment and pesticides. The mangrove swamp can absorb and filter out these pollutants up to a certain point, but that limit is being exceeded.

The Potential for Agriculture and Forestry

As has already been described, the area that IRENA decided to recover contains fertile soil with great agricultural potential, steep lands appropriate for forests and wildlife protection, and mangrove swamps of great importance for fishing and recreation. Such a variety of lands and needs requires an integrated and coherent vision, a general plan of organization.

The goals of the Heroes and Martyrs of Veracruz project are to manage and reduce to tolerable limits the erosion that threatens to destroy

Nicaragua's most productive soils, to reduce the environmental impact of intensive agricultural practices, and to restore and conserve almost 200,000 hectares (770 square miles) of land.

To achieve these goals, we recommended the construction of terraces, dikes, filtration ditches, and irrigation canals, as well as other conservation efforts, to recover the most deteriorated agricultural land. We also recommended that an area of 5,000 hectares (19.29 square miles) be reforested and divided into 2,300 hectares (8.87 square miles) of mountainous land, 2,000 hectares (7.71 square miles) of agricultural land, and 700 hectares (2.7 square miles) of windbreaks.

Since the wildlands help control the erosion and deterioration of natural resources, we recognized the need to plan the management of these areas, to use their products (the wood, fish, salt, and wildlife) rationally, and to promote the development of ecotourism within them. And finally, recognizing that one of the principal enemies of resource conservation is fire, we resolved to combat and prevent forest fires so as to protect approximately 100,000 hectares (386 square miles) of tropical dry forest, especially 9,000 hectares (22,230 acres) covering the Maribios Mountain Range.

The Fundamental Factor: Participation of the People

In all these areas and activities, we need to ensure that at the same time the ecological processes and soil productivity are being restored, the local population is given an opportunity to improve their standard of living and to learn new production techniques appropriate for the ecosystem in which they live.

To this end, and to achieve an effective and permanent change in the unsustainable farming systems employed by the area's campesinos, it is essential that the campesinos actively participate in the new agricultural activities that are being proposed. These include the use of firewood, biogas, and other types of alternative energy; production using agroforestry; fishing, ecotourism, and other projects. Because we also need to make the people aware of the importance of managing the environment well, it was proposed that formal and informal educational activities—courses, workshops, and talks—be organized and that the active participation of the general population—especially that of the rural people—be sought. Finally, it is vital that we maintain a continuous dialogue with the farmers, remain alert to their needs and expectations, and be able to learn from their knowledge and experiences.

For these reasons, IRENA requested the different international organizations interested in financing and coordinating the project's distinct components to let the campesino population carry out the activities, or at least be allowed to participate substantially.

Accordingly, IRENA initiated a series of activities to involve the campesinos in the various alternatives for directly improving their living standards. The farmers began to repair the rural roads, which facilitated access to their villages and the shipping of their crops. They also planted trees on their farms in the form of living fences and windbreaks. Additionally, they eliminated unnecessary applications of pesticides on their crops, saving themselves a great deal of money, while IRENA introduced simple techniques for integrated pest management to cut down on pesticide use even further. New farming techniques were also used to increase productivity, and farmers were provided with better quality seeds to improve their harvest. All these actions were identified, planned, and carried out in close communication with the campesinos.

The first positive results were seen in the pilot project at the Pikín Guerrero cooperative on the slopes of Casita Volcano, which was coordinated by the World Conservation Union (IUCN). From the first year, 1988, production there increased, motivating two neighboring cooperatives to join the activities of conservation and improved agricultural production. In early 1989, three more cooperatives joined the project, and by the end of that year, their number totaled seven. At that point, it was a regional conservation initiative based on campesino participation, to which more land and efforts were being continually added all the time.

During this period, a campesino-to-campesino training system was instituted, in which the instructors were themselves campesinos. The cooperatives that had more experience and had taken part in training workshops taught their companions different techniques, such as how to use an "A" level, how to dig furrows on a graded curve, how to make terraces and filtration ditches, and how to run a vegetable or tree nursery. They also discussed such issues as the best seasons for planting and the more useful species. In short, the training system imparted a collection of methods and information related to conservation and land management that allows the campesinos to resolve their own problems.

This method of transferring technology has proven to be more efficient than traditional methods; the farmers have learned the material better and have been more likely to put the knowledge into practice than when the training comes from technicians from institutions. Moreover, the results achieved through this training have been excellent.

The Women: Source of Action and Motivation for Change

In the campesinos' cultural environment, women play a very significant role. They are an important work force, highly capable of performing certain specialized tasks that men either cannot or will not do. They also receive training more efficiently, and they are more meticulous than men when performing such delicate tasks as managing nurseries or reviewing and controlling pests on the crops.

Furthermore, in education and change at the family level, women are

Photo 5.2 Farmer-to-Farmer Grassroots Education: Popular participation is crucial for the success of the project. Extension services and training are carried out in a farmer-to-farmer program, directly involving participants at the grassroots level. *Credit: Gabriel Travis=no*

indispensable in their ability to exert considerable influence in modifying traditional family behaviors toward certain problems. Thus, they have been able to interest their spouses in alternative solutions that they might not have seen before. And insofar as the cooperatives were able to overcome certain cultural prejudices to support female participation in the decision-making process, many women proposed ideas and initiatives that motivated the men to take specific actions and to involve the entire family in the activities. Today, the participation of women is one of the central components of the project. It has been enthusiastically received by local authorities and by the cooperatives themselves.

Education at the Service of the People

In the work with the community, participation of the universities has also been vital. León is the home of the oldest and most important university in the country: the National Autonomous University of Nicaragua (UNAN). Some problems, those related primarily to biological control of pests in the lands of the cooperatives and to the management and conservation of the mangrove swamps in the project's coastal zone, required the knowledge of academic specialists. Therefore, IRENA invited UNAN's School of Biology to complete scientific studies and design work plans for those areas.

The biology students and their professors initiated the technologically simple design of a system of integrated pest control, which the campesinos easily accepted. This system helped reduce the use of pesticides on their crops, the savings from which have motivated the campesinos to perfect their own methods of pest management and to adopt new techniques for biological control.

Another group of students has been studying the important mangrove estuary ecosystem, which is threatened by overexploitation and the expansion of agricultural land into the area. To develop proposals for the sustainable management of that ecosystem, the students completed inventories and studies of the many traditional uses that the campesinos and fishermen have for the swamp's resources. They have also tried to quantify the productive capacity of those resources to determine permissible quotas for their extraction without degrading them.

At present, these students are experimenting with some combinations of sustainable extraction at various pilot plots, developing methods for promoting natural regeneration and restoring degraded mangroves, as well as alternative uses for certain resources. From these tests, they hope to develop techniques that can later be transferred to the local fishermen and campesinos. This plan will not only prevent the exhaustion of the mangrove swamps' resources but also guarantee their long-term conservation.

Photo 5.3 Mangrove Forest: The Heroes and Martyrs project area stretches from the slopes of the mountains to the mangroves of the Pacific coast. The economic value of the mangroves is recognized by the fishermen. *Credit: Gabriel Travisano*

The Pressures of Economic Growth

The economic policies of Violeta Barrios de Chamorro, who was elected president of Nicaragua in April 1990, seek a substantial increase in exports to correct the financial deficit inherited from years of war and economic blockade. In the area of the project, these policies are reflected in an expansion of the land planted in cotton, the principal agro-export product. The plans indicate a hope to double the area currently planted to 120,000 hectares (460 square miles). This means that some land now dedicated to other crops will give way to cotton, as a result of which even more land in the already deteriorated Pacific region of Nicaragua will be cleared. Worse yet, this implies that the importation and use of chemicals, especially fertilizers and pesticides, will double. If this happens, the effects on the quality of the environment, already extremely contaminated by the accumulation of nondegradable biocides, could be catastrophic.

There are, of course, inherent difficulties in trying to effect an entire transformation in land use and farming technology. The lack of financial resources prevents greater agility and efficiency in the activities of restoration, education, and training. The lack of people trained in the different necessary disciplines and specialties and the continued industrial and domestic demands on the dry forest for firewood have also limited the project's accomplishments. But given that the cultivation of cotton is the region's principal source of soil degradation, water pollution, and deforestation, the goal to increase the area of cotton production completely contradicts the original proposals of the project. Thus, the imperatives of reconstruction and development are exerting more pressure on the area's natural resources, forcing the country to assume the environmental costs of the new economic policies.

A Future of Hope

Despite the difficulties generated by the entire process of change as well as by the urgent need for economic development, the institutions, international organizations, and local inhabitants continue their efforts to meet the planned objectives. More integral and sustainable methods are being developed to extract the resources of the coastal mangrove swamps. Procedures for the application and granting of agricultural credit are being introduced as incentives for farmers to devise techniques to stabilize and conserve soil on agricultural land. New methods for environmental education and technical training are also being developed to improve the capacity of the local populace to carry out conservation programs on their own. Also, women are participating more in solving the problems their communities face, thereby learning the value of their point of view and this productive capacity. And all the time more cooperatives are becoming interested in and integrated into the conservation activities of the steep land in the foothills of the volcanic mountain range.

An example of the continuous efforts of all the area's protagonists is the tiny project to conserve the rare pines of the Casita Volcano. On the slopes of this volcano exists a small forest of *Pinus oocarpa*, the northern-most natural distribution in the Americas of this species of pine. This true ecological curiosity is in danger of disappearing due to forest fires and indiscriminate cutting. However, with the combined efforts of the campesinos, university students, and international support, a small genetic forest reserve will be created to protect those specimens from the forces that threaten them.

These pines are a symbol for the region. Growing in the sandy, infertile soil of the volcanic slope, they seem to demonstrate the enormous capacity of nature to survive in the most adverse conditions. They are also a defiant example of the capacity of the environment to resist the negative effects of uncontrolled human activity. Finally, they are proof that those degraded territories are still capable of regaining their original fertility, returning quality to their waters, and finding a form of sustainable cohabitation between agricultural peoples and their environment.

Like the pines of the Casita Volcano, the inhabitants of the region can demonstrate their ability to confront adversity and triumph over difficulties. One day, regreened slopes may show the world that hope is not lost and that men and women together can restore the resources that they had once pushed to the point of destruction.

6 Jocotal In El Salvador

More Wild Ducks, More Protein for the People

Manuel Benítez Arias

In a large volcanic crater some 30 kilometers (19 miles) from El Salvador's southern coast, in a swampy zone that was once covered with forests, there is an extensive lagoon where, in one day, you can see thousands of black-bellied, whistling, and fulvous ducks. Although the tree duck population is considered to be growing today, this has not always been the case. Many years of hunting in the zone had decreased and nearly eliminated the population of these ducks. Moreover, their nesting sites—natural cavities in trees—were disappearing with the forest. Thus, by 1977, it was estimated that only about 500 whistling ducks remained in the lagoon, and these, too, were in danger of disappearing.

For this reason, the National Parks and Wildlife Service decided in 1976 to introduce a program of protection and conservation at the lagoon. At first, we focused on studying the lagoon's floral and faunal resources, particularly the aquatic birds, and on protecting the area from recreational hunting and illegal logging. Then, upon noting the fragility of the black-bellied tree duck population, we decided to initiate a wild duck management project. This entailed constructing artificial nests, which the ducks quickly accepted.

As the project developed, the people living near the lagoon became more involved, not only in protecting the ducks and other area resources, but also in using some of their "products"; the eggs collected from the nests provided local residents with some of the protein missing from their diet.

As with most Latin American countries, El Salvador's wilderness resources have, since pre-Columbian times, been an important source of food and construction supplies for rural populations. The wild fauna, in particular, has been a major source of animal protein for campesinos.

Today, protein continues to be an urgent need for Salvadorans. Malnutrition affects more than 65 percent of the children and the average consumption of meat is less than the minimum requirement stipulated by both the Nutritional Institute of Central America and Panama and the World Health Organization.

In addition to the malnutrition problems, El Salvador suffers from

high rates of illiteracy and deficient basic services, especially in the areas of health and education. And the ever-present military violence and frequent armed conflicts have tortured the country for many years. These conditions of poverty, illiteracy, health and diet problems, and frequent violence are mirrored in the small population living in the neighborhood of El Jocotal lagoon.

In the face of all this adversity, the wild duck management project has provided some measures of success. Along with the ecological benefits it has brought, such as the restoration of a resident population of whistling ducks, the project has also brought social benefits to the people of El Jocotal—namely, training in various conservation activities and the consumption of 30,000 eggs, which has helped alleviate the widespread malnutrition in the area.

Where El Jocotal Fits In

The republic of El Salvador is the smallest country in Latin America, with a territory of only 21,400 square kilometers (8,260 square miles) and one of the highest population densities on the continent (218 inhabitants per square kilometer, or 671 inhabitants per square mile). It also has one of the highest demographic growth rates in the world (3.6 percent annually, 1985).

According to the Salvadoran Forest Service, only 12 percent of the territory is covered with trees and only 3 percent can be considered in a wild state. The wetlands, such as the mangroves, swamps, and tidal zones, are under increasing pressure from extreme deforestation, drainage, eutrophication, and pollution.

El Jocotal is part of the El Transito Municipality, San Miguel Department, which is located 17 kilometers (10.5 miles) south-southeast of the city of San Miguel. The lagoon lies about 20 meters (66 feet) above sea level in a valley bordered by the Chaparrastique, or San Miguel, volcano on the north and by the Jucuarán Hills on the south. Its size varies from 500 hectares (1.92 square miles) during the dry season to 1,500 hectares (5.78 square miles) during the rainy season. Its average depth fluctuates between 1.5 meters (5 feet) during the dry season to 3 meters (10 feet) during the rainy season, and it reaches even greater depths at small springs near the northern shore.

The zone is classified as subtropical moist forest, according to the Holdridge classification. Annual precipitation is about 1,750 millimeters (68 inches), with an average temperature of 26 degrees Celsius (79 degrees Fahrenheit) and an average relative humidity of 70 percent.

El Jocotal is located south of the San Miguel volcano, separated from the coast by the Jucuarán Mountain Range (Figure 6.1). The waters that feed the lagoon flow out the lake bottom after having been absorbed by the recent lava flows of the volcano.

Figure 6.1   El Jocotal Lagoon

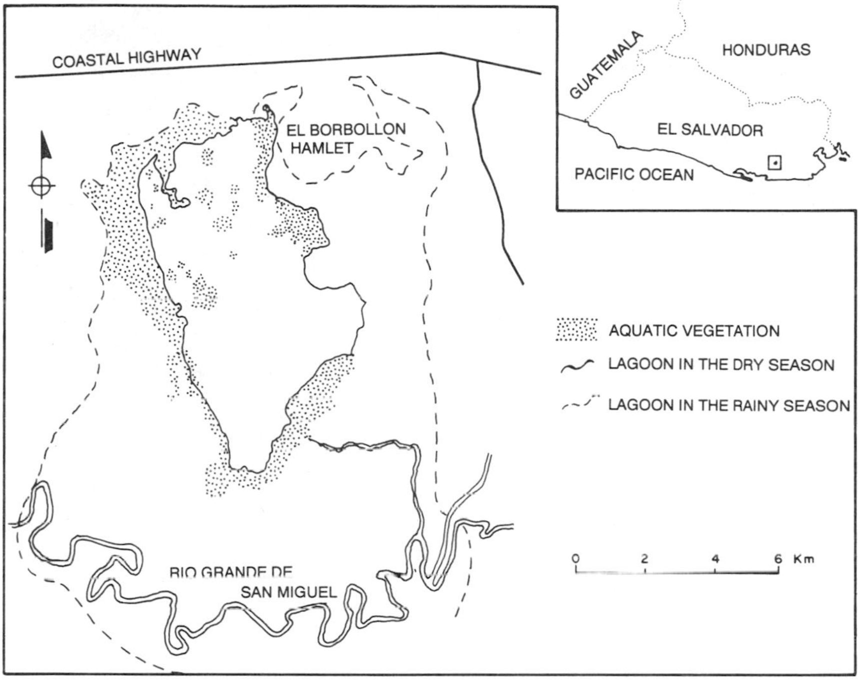

This hot zone was once surrounded by a swampy forest. But that forest has now been almost completely eliminated to create pastures and cotton fields and, recently, to plant watermelon and cantaloupe. Nevertheless, along the edge of the San Miguel River, which feeds the lagoon during the rainy season, there still remain plots of muddy forest that house birds, butterflies, and rich vegetation.

El Jocotal lagoon attracted the attention of the National Parks and Wildlife Service because of its biological importance. It has an enormous diversity of aquatic plants and birds, and is the most important body of water in El Salvador that serves as a resting point for birds migrating from North America.

Natural Wealth, Human Poverty

The lagoon contains all kinds of aquatic plant life. More than 60 different species jut out of the water, float on the surface, remain submerged in, or stand along the margins of El Jocotal.

The submerged vegetation predominates, forming a dense platform on the surface where aquatic birds can walk and rest without sinking. The most abundant species are the hydrillas (*Hydrilla verticillata*), 'coon tails (*Ceratophyllum demersum*), and water nymphs (*Najas*). Plants like water

Photo 6.1   Aquatic Migratory Bird in El Jocotal: Thousands of aquatic migratory and resident birds benefit from the vegetation of the lagoon. El Jocotal is the most important body of water in El Salvador in the migratory route origination in the Northern Hemisphere. *Credit: Manuel Benítez Arias*

lilies (*Nymphaea ampla*) represent the emergent vegetation.

The water hyacinth (*Eichhornia crassipes*) constitutes the most numerous floating plant. Water lettuce (*Pistia stratiotes*), duck weeds (*Salvinia, Lemna,* and *Spirodela*), and mosquito ferns (*Azolla caroliniana*) are also common.

Advancing from the lagoon's edge, the reeds (*Phragmites cummunis*), cattails (*Typha angustifolia*), and water potatoes (*Sagittaria lancifolia*) have invaded the watery domain.

The forest that once surrounded the lagoon has almost completely disappeared. There remain only dispersed trees, like the rain tree, or monkeypod (*Pithecolobium saman*), ceiba tree (*Ceiba pentandra*), pimiento (*Phyllanthus elsiae*), and papalón (*Coccoloba carcasana*).

Wildlife of the Lagoon

More than 130 species of aquatic birds can be found amid the lagoon's thick vegetation. Some of these spend their lives at El Jocotal, as is the case with some threatened species that maintain stable populations at the lagoon. Others, as noted above, use it as a rest stop on their migratory route from the Northern Hemisphere.

Among the resident birds, wild ducks abound. In El Jocotal one can find black-bellied tree ducks (*Dendrocygna autumnalis*), fulvous ducks (*D. bicolor*), masked ducks (*Oxyura dominicana*), and Muscovy ducks (*Cairina moschata*). These last two have nearly disappeared from other sites in El Salvador.

The lagoon is also home for such birds as the green heron (*Butorides virescens*), the American coot (*Fulica americana*), the common stilt (*Himantopus himantopus*), the northern jacana (*Jacana spinosa*), the least grebe (*Tachybaptus dominicanus*), and the pied-billed grebe (*Podilymbus podiceps*).

During the dry season, from November to March, the lagoon is visited by migratory birds, such as the blue-winged teal (*Anas discors*), the northern shoveler (*A. clypeata*), the American wigeon (*A. americana*), and the lesser scaup (*Aythya affinis*).

Although birds abound, terrestrial fauna is scarce. Hunting, combined with the disappearance of natural habitat, has put continuous pressure on the fragile populations. A small body of crocodiles (*Crocodylus acutus*) persists, and iguanas (*Iguana iguana*), ctenosaur lizards (*Ctenosaura similis*), and boas (*Boa constrictor*) can still be found in the lagoon's surroundings.

The Neighbors of El Jocotal

Some 1,500 people live near El Jocotal year round. In addition, during the harvest seasons for cotton, cantaloupe, and watermelon, a migrant population appears in the region.

The people around El Jocotal live in conditions that border on misery.

More than 65 percent of the population do not know how to read or write. They barely have access to minimal health and education facilities. The lack of running water and a sewage system forces them to use the lagoon and the nearby San Miguel River to wash their clothes, bathe, discharge their waste, and obtain drinking water for their families.

In the small settlement of El Borbollon, on the northern edge of the lagoon, live some 300 families of meager resources. The lowlands they occupy do not have an owner. During the rainy season this land is often flooded, which forces the residents to break down the fences of a private farm situated on a nearby hill and temporarily squat on that land.

The neighbors of El Jocotal live exclusively by agriculture and fishing. They mainly plant corn, sorgum, watermelon, and cotton. To complement these few crops, they fish for two or three species, among them the tiger *guapote*, which was brought from Nicaragua and introduced in the lagoon, and which today represents a veritable plague because it has eliminated all the local predators.

Their principal source of energy is firewood, which they gather from the scarce trees in their surroundings. Their primary source of water and food is the lagoon. During the dry season, El Jocotal provides water for the survival of up to 1,000 people in the surrounding area.

The Rescue of the Whistling Ducks

When the National Parks and Wildlife Service arrived at El Jocotal lagoon in March 1976, a tourism business that brought hunters from the United States was operating in the area. Upon establishment of the Wildlife Reserve, hunting for sport as well as deforestation were prohibited. To enforce this prohibition and to protect the lake and its resources, we established a small corps of forest guards, recruiting personnel who were receptive to the ideas and conservation objectives of the service and who had a positive attitude about the role they would have to play. These guards were selected from among inhabitants of the zone; in fact they were the same people who had worked as guides for the foreign hunters. From the time of their recruitment, incidents of poaching decreased.

From the beginning, we also employed the forest guards as assistants in the research and wildlife management projects that were being undertaken. This experience improved their training in the field.

During the first two years, research was focused on biological studies of the lagoon, particularly of the aquatic birds. We then decided to establish an experimental project in which nesting boxes would be installed for the black-bellied whistling ducks.

The project began with the construction of artificial nests made of boards from the earfruit tree (*Enterolobium cyclocarpum*), a relatively scarce and expensive wood that was chosen for its durability and resistance to

Photo 6.2 Park Rangers Surveying El Jocotal Lagoon: During the first years of its presence in El Jocotal, the National Parks Service concentrated its efforts on research and protection of the area. As a result, they were able to document the sharp decrease in the tree-duck population. *Credit: Manuel Benítez Arias*

bad weather. In designing the nests, we applied what had been learned through experience in the reproduction of another tree-duck species in the southwestern United States. This was the first time that artificial nests were used for the reproduction of wild ducks in El Salvador, however, and we adapted our dimensions and designs according to the size of various natural tree-duck nests found at El Jocotal.

Due to the extensive deforestation around the lagoon, the need for nesting sites was so great that as early as 1977, the project's first year, the ducks used more than half the artificial residences (forty-six of the eighty boxes constructed). That year, some 800 ducklings were born.

In the following three years, more than 150 boxes were installed on the trunks of dead and living trees and on wooden posts. They were placed near the edge of the lagoon, both amid existing vegetation and in unpopulated fields, and always within 300 meters (985 feet) of the water. The boxes were installed at different distances and heights (between 7 and 9 meters [23–30 feet]), depending on the available trees. There were from 3 to 25 boxes per hectare, and in some trees up to 10 boxes were installed. Every 14 days the boxes would be checked. In some, the eggs of only one female were found; in others, there was collective nesting.

The results reported by Gómez (1986) indicate that, in the period 1977–81, the boxes were used 83.8 percent of time during the reproductive period, from May to December.

Of the 825 nests studied, 268 were individual and 557 were collective nests.

The incubation period was 29 ±3.5 days, and the nests contained 49 ±25 eggs, with an average of 30 ±19 ducklings born from each nest, mainly during the month of October.

To obtain information about possible terrestrial predators, the nests were left completely unprotected. The most important predators were found to be the four-eyed opossum (*Philander opossum*) and the boa.

Military violence during the following years (1981–85) ended up eliminating the remaining trees in the zone. We then began placing nesting boxes on posts to see if the ducks would accept such artificial structures. Not only did they accept them, but they occupied almost all of the 400 boxes installed. And when the boxes were not occupied by whistling ducks, they were used as refuges and nesting sites by other species, such as the tropical horned owl (*Otus*) and the four-eyed opossum.

For the Good of the People: Protein and Education

During this period, it was noted that sometimes as many as 100 eggs could be found in one box due to multiple nesting. Many of these eggs were lost because the female was unable to keep them warm. From this observation came the idea of offering eggs to the community for their

Photo 6.3 Artificial Tree-duck Nest: Artificial nests, designed according to the size of natural nests of the black bellied tree-ducks, were nailed to tree trunks or wooden posts. The ducks readily accepted this new nesting option.
Credit: Manuel Benítez Arias

consumption. The people of the area were already accustomed to eating duck eggs and meat, so the offer was well received. Thus, the project's neighbors increased their consumption of protein and were converted to a sympathetic force for the project and for conservation activities at the lagoon.

Also during this period, the National Parks and Wildlife Service began to participate in the Program of Employment Generation, with the financial support of the U.S. Agency for International Development (USAID) and the government of El Salvador. This program sought to alleviate the problems stemming from the country's social and political situation.

The financing provided to the service permitted us to establish twelve projects for the creation of protected natural areas and thirty-eight projects for wildlife management. The wild duck management project at El Jocotal used the new funds for 300 nesting boxes. From the new boxes installed between 1981 and 1985, over 30,000 eggs were harvested (the majority by the local population) and over 12,000 ducklings were born.

More than ninety people, hired from the local community, participated directly or indirectly in the project's activities. When the financing ran out, all these people had already been trained, as can be seen in the fact that some have constructed nesting boxes near their houses and have harvested them with surprising success. This has contributed to their better appreciation of the natural resources and beauty of the lagoon, stimulating their participation in the protection of such a valuable wildlife refuge.

Small Victories

Nevertheless, problems still exist. During the dry season, the water level drops, allowing private property lines to extend to the border of the lagoon. The owners of cattle ranches have taken advantage of this situation to expand their farms farther to the south. Later, when the waters rise again, the ranchers sometimes drain the lagoon to keep their new land, thus acquiring more land every year and putting more pressure on the resources.

At the same time, nearby crops such as cotton and vegetables use large quantities of pesticides, which are washed into the lagoon via the San Miguel River. These threaten the survival not only of the aquatic species but also of the local population.

To all this is added the fact that, during the last 10 years, the zone has constantly been subjected to problems of violence and armed conflict. The resultant insecurity has made it difficult to undertake any type of continuous action to protect the lagoon or improve the fragile situation of its inhabitants.

Nevertheless, through the wild duck management project, protein consumption has been increased for a population that lives in precarious conditions. For people in any but the most dire straits of poverty and malnutrition, the consumption of 30,000 eggs would seem to bring modest relief. For the inhabitants of El Jocotal, however, it is significant, and they have benefited greatly from this new source of sustenance.

Furthermore, until 1985 there had been few opportunities for formal training of technical or professional personnel in the country. With the practical experience obtained at El Jocotal, however, a large number of technicians, professionals and campesinos acquired training that could be useful for work in this same field or in other situations.

Finally, in the area of ecology, the wild duck management project has succeeded in achieving the rapid and surprising restoration of a resident population of ducks that was disappearing due to indiscriminate hunting and the lack of nesting sites. Moreover, our successes in El Jocotal have been reproduced in two other areas with similar conditions—that is, wetlands with populations of the same duck species. These areas are the mangroves of Barra de Santiago in the Ahuachapan Department and the Island of San Sebastián, with its swamps and beaches. The application of the technology developed in El Jocotal has been particularly successful in San Sebastián, where they are also using the boxes experimentally for such species as the Muscovy duck (*Cairina moschata*) and the yellow-crowned parrot (*Amazona ochrocephala*). Thus, the technology that was developed has proven not only reproducible but also adaptable for other species, though with a few modifications. And the project has also permitted scientists to compile basic biological information about important aspects of the management of wild ducks.

The nests that were installed during the first years of the project will permit us to continue raising whistling ducks in the region for many years to come. So it is that, every afternoon, upon seeing thousands of whistling ducks fly over the water of El Jocotal lagoon, the local people will know not only that they are assured a source of protein but also that their children will be able to enjoy that wealth of food and natural beauty.

7 Monterrico

A Reserve for Maximum Use

Juan Carlos Godoy

On the central Pacific coast of Guatemala, a busy community of some 2,000 fisherpeople, salt collectors, wood collectors, and charcoal makers live off the rich resources offered by the small Monterrico Nature Reserve. This sun-baked stretch of intricate mangrove swamps and scenic beaches is the site of an exceptional example of protected zone management.

Monterrico is a beautiful area with 2,800 hectares (10.8 square miles) of beaches, coastal lagoons, and mangrove swamps, all of which serve as reproductive and hatching zones for crabs, mollusks, shrimp, and fish with commercial value. Iguanas, turtles, caimans, and numerous bird colonies also live there. Thus, the reserve holds great scientific value as well, not only because it serves the traditional functions of a mangrove swamp (fish hatchery, animal habitat, stabilization of the coastal border, and so on) but also because of its notable biological diversity. Finally, Monterrico has recreational value as it offers a weekend escape for thousands of city dwellers who flock there to get away from the noise, air pollution, and crowds of the capital.

Yet few people appreciate the economic and scientific value of the mangrove swamps, and most continually exploit the swamps to extract firewood, tannins, and materials for construction and making charcoal. As a result, the areas of mangroves and associated wetlands in Guatemala have been disappearing at an alarming rate. Between 1960 and 1985, Guatemala, which has coasts on both the Pacific Ocean and Caribbean Sea, saw half of its 500 square kilometers (193 square miles) of mangroves destroyed.

In recognition of both its value and its peril, the Monterrico Nature Reserve was created in 1977 by means of a presidential accord, which destined it "for the protection of the fauna and flora, and generally, of the natural ecosystem of estuaries and natural lagoons." Since then, Monterrico has been administered by the Center for Conservation Studies (CECON) of the University of San Carlos in collaboration with the Ministry of Agriculture.

In the beginning, the reserve served exclusively as a site for research. In 1984, however, under pressure from neighboring populations who

88

depend on the mangrove's resources for their daily subsistence, CECON began to design a project proposal for management of the zone. Up to this time, reserves were managed as if no one lived in them. But because Monterrico is a populated area with complex economic dynamics, we wanted to try a type of integrated management that would consider the beaches, mangroves, and lagoons together with their fishermen, charcoal makers, and weekend visitors.

Thus, while the local people exploit the wood, fish, tourism, and other products of Monterrico, CECON, an ecological organization, administers the reserve with a philosophy that is novel for the country. There is no attempt to enclose the zone in a crystal ball so that it may only be viewed from afar without touching. Instead, the zone is managed with a dynamic vision that promotes local participation in all conservation activities and recognizes the local population's need to use the reserve's resources.

The Living Reserve

Guatemala, in the extreme north of Central America, is the region's most populated nation, with 9.3 million inhabitants who speak 19 indigenous languages, as well as Spanish. Forty-five percent of its population is younger than 15 years old.

Of its 108,800 square kilometers (42,000 square miles), 82 percent is mountainous. This terrain includes 33 volcanoes. Annual precipitation varies between 350 and 6,500 millimeters (14–254 inches) in altitudes that range from sea level to above 4,000 meters (13,000 feet). All this variety creates the conditions for at least 12 life zones.

The Monterrico Nature Reserve, located 125 kilometers (77.5 miles) from Guatemala City via paved road, is on the Pacific Coast, within the municipalities of Taxisco and Chiquimulilla in the Santa Rosa Department. It is in an area bordered by the Oliveros River, the Chiquimulilla Canal, and La Palmilla lagoon (Figure 7.1).

The reserve, which is between 0 and 5 meters (0–16 feet) above sea level, comprises the lower stretches of two watersheds: that of the Maria Linda River, which is 88 kilometers (55 miles) long and that of the Paso Hondo River, which is 240 kilometers (150 miles) long. Before flowing into the Pacific Ocean, both rivers form an ecosystem of estuaries and coastal lagoons, which change daily and annually in relative salinity.

The average annual temperature of the reserve is 26 degrees Celsius (79 degrees Fahrenheit), with an average annual precipitation of about 1,530 millimeters (59.7 inches), an average annual relative humidity of 84 percent, and average annual winds of 17.4 kilometers (10.8 miles) per hour north-northeast.

The zone is classified according to the Holdridge system as Subtropical Dry Forest Transitional to Moist.

Figure 7.1 Monterrico Nature Reserve

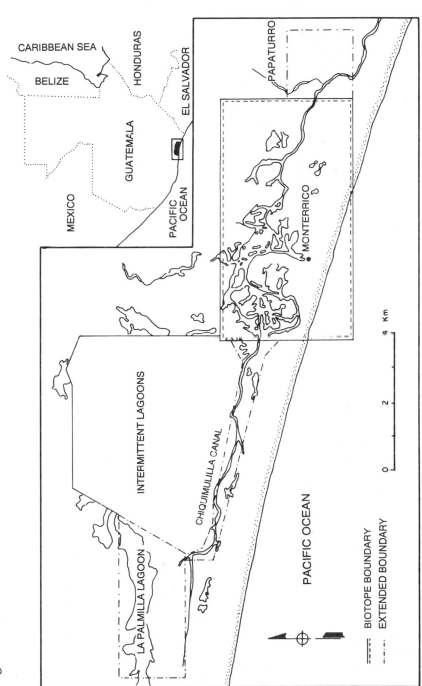

Beaches, Mangroves, and Plovers

During six months of the year—November to April—the beaches of Monterrico bake in the summer sun. This is the dry season; few rains refresh the zone, and the water recedes to leave the roots of the mangroves uncovered. From May to October, on the other hand, frequent rains pound down over the silvery sands, and water once again fills the canals that weave between the spiderlike roots of the mangroves. Because the flat alluvial soils of Monterrico do not have a good system for draining the quantities of water that fall during the winter, the zone is constantly flooded.

According to the most recent research within the reserve, Monterrico contains at least five vegetational formations: mangrove forests, dry forests, riverbank forests, marshes, and aquatic vegetation.

On the trails of Monterrico, one can see the gourd tree (*Crescentia*), with its branches that imitate a green glass of wine, together with the thick, horn-shaped thorns of the ant acacia (*Acacia*). During the dry season, the coppery reflections from the bark of the *jiñocuave* (*Bursera*), or naked Indian, shine beneath the ardent sun.

Still, the characteristic image of Monterrico is the mangrove forest. The red mangrove (*Rhizophora*) thrusts its roots down into the mud and water while the black mangrove (*Avicennia*) pokes root appendages up from the water and mud to breathe. Also abundant are white mangroves (*Laguncularia*) and herbaceous plants such as the cattails (*Typha*), water hyacinths (*Eichhornia* and *Nymphaea*), and aquatic ferns (*Pistia*).

As for wild fauna, the reserve is home for countless species. The dominant fauna—also the most diverse and attractive—are the birds. Between residents and migratory visitors, there are more than 100 species of birds in Monterrico, including pelicans (*Pelicanidae*), herons (*Ardeidae*), ducks (*Anatidae*), plovers (*Charadriidae*), osprey (*Pandionidae*), hawks (*Falconidae*), rails (*Rallidae*), and parakeets (*Psittacidae*).

Of great interest for the local people are the numerous marine species, such as shrimp (*Penaeus* and *Macrobrachium*), crabs (*Callinectes*), and conchs (*Crassostrea*), that are found in the mangrove swamps and beaches. Commercial fish abound; at least twenty-six species are known, among them mullet (*Mugilidae*), cichlids (*Chiclasoma*), snook (*Centropomus*), and four-eyed fish (*Anableps*).

On the trails one hears the rustling of leaves as iguanas (*Iguana*), ctenosaurs (*Ctenosaura*), and boas (*Boa loxocemus*) scurry and slither away. At least ten species of reptiles have been sighted; notable among them is a small population of caimans (*Crocodilus*). In addition, at least three species of sea turtles lay their eggs on the beaches of Monterrico.

The mammals, which at one time were abundant, are so threatened today that only opossum (*Didelphis marsupialis*), white-tailed deer (*Odocoileus virginianus*), brocket deer (*Mazama americana*), raccoon (*Procyon lotor*), and coatimundi (*Nasua narica*) remain.

Photo 7.1   Mangrove Forest: Although the Natural Reserve of Monterrico is best known for its beaches, the most notable feature is the mangrove forest.
Credit: Valerie Barzetti

The Human Factor: Residential and Recreational

Within the reserve and in its surroundings are at least 10 villages with anywhere from 80 to 700 inhabitants each. These inhabitants, who are primarily mestizo (of mixed European and native ancestry), began to migrate into the area about 60 years ago. Since then, a continuous flow of people has moved in and out of the region.

Although the standard of living of the local populace is not the highest in the country, neither is the zone impoverished. Some 55 percent of the population can read, and there is a school and a health center, as well as electricity.

Further, there is generally no hunger around Monterrico, thanks to the richness of the ecosystem. Some of the land allows for the cultivation of such products as sesame, corn, beans, watermelon, peppers, hibiscus, *jocote*, tamarind, mango, rice, and palms. There is also, although only to a small degree, some animal husbandry—barely twenty head of beef cattle, hogs, and poultry, which are raised primarily for domestic consumption.

Since both the agriculture and animal husbandry use traditional technology, without machinery or irrigation, and since few farmers use fertilizers or pesticides, the activities that have the biggest impact on the wildlands are fishing and firewood collection. Firewood, which is used in wood-burning ovens to extract salt from water, continues to be the principal fuel in the region. During the dry season, about eight salt ovens operate in the reserve.

Added to the resident population are the thousands of Guatemalans for whom Monterrico is a recreational center, thanks to its scenic beauty, accessibility, and proximity to the capital. In recent years, the demand for beachfront property to construct cabins, hotels, restaurants, and other tourist facilities has noticeably increased. Most of the reserve's visitors arrive during the dry season. Between March and June of 1987, more than 32,000 people entered the reserve; in the month of April alone, almost 16,000 visitors arrived there, mostly on weekends. During the rainy season, on the other hand, few people can be seen on the beaches.

A Master Plan for Management

The Monterrico Nature Reserve was created to protect an ecosystem, and that is how it was first managed. But very soon, the characteristics of the region showed that it was not possible to continue conserving it without considering the local population. Therefore, a master plan was begun in 1984 for the integrated management of the zone, and that plan is still being revised.

The Grand Design

In 1987 CECON began the actual management of the reserve, with the technical collaboration of the Center for Oceanic and Aquacultural Studies (CEMA), the National Forestry Institute (INAFOR, today DIGEBOS), and the Guatemalan Tourism Institute (INGUAT). The World Conservation Union (IUCN) and the Tropical Agricultural Center for Research and Education (CATIE) provide technical and economic support, while the World Wildlife Fund (WWF) is managing the funding for the first phase of basic development.

To administer the reserve, CECON has some basic infrastructure: a rustic house to accommodate six researchers, sanitary services, electricity, a small boat, and minimal laboratory facilities. Personnel consists of a resident biologist and three field workers. We also rely on biology students who volunteer their time so we can initiate detailed inventories and complete environmental education and training programs.

Through the master plan, we have tried to convert Monterrico into a model for the management of other similar reserves. First, the area is representative of ecosystems common to the coastal zones of Guatemala— and perhaps to other regions in Central America—as much for the resources it contains as for the pressures that affect it. Second, the reserve is the primary source of natural products—namely, fish and firewood—for the local population, which makes it the basis of the domestic economy. Third, it is an accessible site, which facilitates not only the constant presence of researchers from such institutions as the University of San Carlos, which manages a branch of CEMA there, but also the environmental education of the thousands of visitors who arrive at its beaches every week.

The master plan is designed to promote the sustainable use of the mangrove forests in a manner that allows the local population's needs to be met while the regenerative capacity of the ecosystem is maintained. To accomplish this, it is considered essential that the inhabitants participate in the conservation of the mangrove swamp and its resources. And because environmental education is a vital tool for enlisting this participation, recreational and interpretive activities that serve this purpose are made available to both residents and weekend visitors. In addition, it is also important that the inhabitants benefit from the swamp's products. Since this requires that the production techniques the farmers use do not damage the environment, the plan suggests supporting the use of alternative agricultural systems wherever harmful techniques are in use.

Even though the plan is not yet finished, Monterrico is already considered a multiple-use area. This definition implies that the area is divided into different zones of use: one for private use, which is urban or agricultural; one for intensive (high-impact) public use; one for extensive public use; and a nucleus that mixes areas of recuperation and absolute protection.

The absolute protection zone includes sites where birds and turtles nest, and other areas of scientific or social interest that are considered fragile. By protecting these sites, we hope to guarantee the production of fish, lobsters, shrimp, conch, and other marine fauna. We have also decided to promote research at these sites, especially concerning endangered species.

The experience of managing a reserve as a multiple-use area is new for CECON, which, as already noted, had always worked exclusively with ecological reserves or wildlife sanctuaries without involving popular participation and, above all, without specifically considering the need of neighboring populations to use the natural resources. Monterrico is, in this sense, a conservation challenge in Guatemala.

Education and Collaboration

CECON has already begun to put some of the master plan's recommendations into practice, mainly those dealing with environmental education and public relations. To date we have run two radio campaigns, an ecology course for the area's schoolteachers, a painting contest, children's games, and workshops for children that deal with the value of natural resources and the need to make sustainable use of them.

This program has been very successful. By introducing multiple and sustainable use of resources through the children, CECON has been able to break the ice and continue working with the other neighboring groups. As part of the same program, we designed and opened two aquatic trails

Photo 7.2   Salt Mining in Monterrico: The reserve continues to be a main source of natural resources for the nearby community and the base of its economy. Salt miners, fishermen, wood collectors, and charcoal makers all depend on the resources of Monterrico. *Credit: Enrique Lahmann*

within the system of rivers and coastal lagoons for weekend visitors to use, and we published two simple folders about the reserve and the trails. In addition, INGUAT has included the reserve in its regional tourist maps, and we posted signs on the highway at the entrance to the reserve. We have also mounted two poster expositions about the area's most outstanding resources, and an audiovisual display has been produced that is constantly being shown to the public. Moreover, the boat operators who ferry visitors to the beaches, pointing out some of the area's abundant birds along the way, have been collaborating with CECON to ensure that the visitors respect certain rules within the reserve and do not throw their garbage into the water.

Prominent among the activities aimed at ensuring local participation in the management of Monterrico was the First Mobile Workshop for local authorities and administrative personnel. The workshop took place in April 1987 with financing from the WWF. Participants visited other protected areas in the country to share their experiences in managing such zones. They also received theoretical training about protected wildland management, conservation as a development strategy, and the technical management of garbage. Finally, they discussed ways to improve conditions for tourism, the philosophy of wildlife protection, and other similar themes. The workshop, in which even the area's mayor participated, was a success and ensured not only the cooperation of local authorities but also the interest and participation of rangers in the conservation of the region's riches.

The collaboration that is expected from local authorities and groups like the Boy Scouts, as well as from associations of boat operators and fisherpeople, will permit us to carry out some of our tasks in vigilance and control. To this end, we have already constructed a visitor checkpoint and an entrance house.

Despite what we have accomplished, exploitation of the mangrove forest for firewood persists, in some cases damaging the resource to such a degree that its subsistence is threatened. Thus, even though we have obtained the collaboration of neighbors such as the boat operators, this assistance is fragile and requires constant educational refreshment to maintain local interest in protecting the resources.

Research and Conservation

Although the emphasis in its master plan is on the use of resources, CECON has effectively maintained its research and conservation work in Monterrico. The reserve already has information about its birds, reptiles, fish, and aquatic plants. Thus, the priority areas in research include a study of the reproductive cycles of shrimp and fish; a study of vegetal succession in estuary forests; socioeconomic research in the use of natural resources such as firewood and palms; and the raising of iguanas, caimans, and turtles in captivity.

Between January and July of 1987, CECON began to experiment with raising iguanas in captivity. A technology was developed to facilitate reproduction in captivity and to ensure the feeding and management of more than 200 animals that were born at the site. In addition to developing, analyzing, and successfully using an appropriate diet, the experiments revealed forms of predation that had never before been reported: for example, snakes were reaching the iguana eggs through subterranean tunnels and certain birds were eating the recently hatched lizards. Some local groups, attracted by the project, constructed their own iguana hatcheries.

The University of San Carlos had a small turtle hatchery in the reserve, which awakened so much interest among local inhabitants that the university decided to move it closer to the beach for easier access. With the support of the community, they managed to release more than 7,000 turtles during the 1987 season.

Unfortunately, although the collection, consumption, and commercialization of turtle eggs are prohibited by law in Guatemala, the reserve's neighbors regularly collect, consume, and sell the turtle eggs during the nesting season. We therefore arranged with them that, for every 100 eggs collected, they would donate between 24 and 48 to the turtle hatchery for incubation and subsequent release. The project was so successful that the

Photo 7.3   Collecting Eggs from a Turtle Hatchery: The small turtle hatchery at the San Carlos University aroused so much community interest that it had to be relocated near the beach. Community members participate regularly in collecting the eggs, a portion of which they donate to the hatchery. Afterwards, they help to release the turtles. *Credit: Juan Carlos Godoy*

Ministry of Agriculture provided funding to some local groups and private farmers to stimulate the creation of new hatcheries. It also prepared a guide for the development and maintenance of turtle hatcheries.

Monterrico Toward the Future

To consolidate what we have already achieved in managing the reserve and to increase community awareness, we must continue our initial work and extend it to certain crucial areas. Such areas include the training of technicians, consciousness raising for resident populations, and environmental education for visitors.

To increase community participation in the programs of the university, we need to strengthen activities in environmental education of residents and begin training the reserve's neighbors in the management of Monterrico's wildlife (such as iguanas, caimans, turtles, deer, and *tepezcuintles*).

In the area of research, our priorities are to study both the resources that are exposed to the greatest pressures and the environmental impact of agricultural activity and annual fires on the seasonal swamps and critical nesting and feeding zones of species that are threatened or in danger of extinction. We also propose compiling an inventory of the area's resources, with emphasis on those in highest demand by the neighboring populations; studying the population dynamics of the fish and birds most consumed; establishing an agroforestry model for the dune zone; and developing alternatives such as solar energy for activities that now demand large quantities of firewood.

Finally, we are working to complete the management plan. Among other things, this means establishing a system for patrolling the mangrove and swamp zones of the reserve, as well as other sites considered important; constructing a visitors' center that would provide information about the reserve's natural resources; and designing programs directed toward Monterrico's weekend visitors.

The work in the Monterrico Nature Reserve has opened doors to a new vision of conservation in Guatemala. The example it has set—that of a single site that accommodates scientists and wood collectors, ecologists and fisherpeople, park rangers and tourists, students and salt collectors, all enjoying the same riches and living in harmony—has shown that it is

The final paragraph on page 99 ends as follows:

... possible to develop a community without destroying the ecosystem on which its survival is based.

— erratum to *Toward a Green Central America*

8 | Toward a Green Central America

Carlos Quesada Mateo

Central America is a land of contrasts, as evidenced by its wide variety of climates, geography, geological formations, topography, and peoples, as well as its extraordinary biodiversity. Sadly, the contrasts are also profound on the socioeconomic and political levels. In general, the abyss between the haves and the have-nots is rapidly widening; the reasons for this are the lack of visionary political decisions, an internal resistance to social justice, the accelerated deterioration of essential ecological processes, the unfavorable terms of international commercial exchange, and the meddling of external forces that foment fratricidal disputes. Despite this gloomy and convulsive panorama, colleagues in the different Central American countries have offered encouraging responses through innovative case studies. Some of those responses are presented in this book.

Guillermo Archibold eloquently narrates a story that speaks for itself. The way of life in the Kuna Yala region constitutes a complete school of thought regarding the relationship between humans and nature. We can learn much from this vision. That indigenous community represents a people who, while resisting being culturally absorbed, have incorporated valuable scientific and technological tools from what they call "the strange culture" and have looked for support to activate a shared responsibility in defense of the environment.

In the case of La Tigra National Park, Rigoberto Romero Meza and Francisco Martínez Gallegos present one of the best examples of the compatibility of conservation and development. A small park of 7,600 hectares (nearly 29 square miles) of cloud forest contributes almost 40 percent of the water for Tegucigalpa, the capital of Honduras. The water is obtained at a treatment cost that is twenty-three times lower than the cost for water from the Guacerique River, which has been degraded by deforestation and various types of contaminants. The economic value and importance of La Tigra—originally protected for its natural riches—noticeably increase if one considers the savings in water treatment and operation costs and the incalculable benefits the park provides for hundreds of thousands of people in the city.

With her professional studies in tourism administration and her practical experiences in natural resources development, Tamara Budowski has successfully mastered the field of nature tourism. Her exposition clearly shows the wide-ranging importance of a system of natural parks and protected areas. In addition to their intrinsic ecological value, these protected areas contain the raw material for the development of a new, vigorous entrepreneurial activity that generates foreign exchange, creates employment, assists conservation, and permits diverse options for environmental education.

In the case of Nicaragua, Lorenzo Cardenal illustrates some of the options for and restrictions to organizing land use in one of the most active agricultural zones on the country's Pacific side. The massive planting of windbreaks to prevent wind erosion while ensuring diverse possibilities for land use was particularly successful. The search for multiple-use management and the enlistment of popular participation were determining factors in the process.

Manuel Benítez Arias shows that even in very adverse conditions, it has been possible to integrate scientific work with the daily occupations of inhabitants of a densely populated zone that is subject to extreme poverty. The efforts he describes permitted the rescue of a threatened duck species and, at the same time, contributed a source of important protein to the population. These efforts, the success of which depended on preliminary research and community participation, thus created an awareness of the ecological value of a lagoon that accommodates some 130 bird species.

Juan Carlos Godoy focuses his study on the Monterrico estuary and its mangrove swamp, one of the most threatened and least valued ecosystems in Central America. His case demonstrates how the swamp contributes to the sustainable development of the region by permitting the coastal communities to use it as a source of employment and subsistence while aiding in its conservation.

All these examples constitute a faith-inspiring catalog of the numerous possibilities that exist for pursuing environmental conservation through concrete actions while trying to achieve sustainable development. These possibilities exist in a region where, scarcely 15 years ago, an environmental movement began. Since then, after conquering multiple obstacles and through the power of necessity, that movement has been notably strengthened. Today it is taking its first steps on the level of regional integration, and it must enrich, multiply, and renovate itself in order to be, as the Spanish philosopher Ortega y Gasset said, at "the height of the times." It is worth reflecting upon the regional and world contexts of the Central American environmental movement, which is linked to a long-term vision and stems from the concepts of shared responsibility and solidarity in the ecological field.

In a world that continues to be economically, politically, and environmentally fragile in the midst of a dizzying explosion of knowledge, communication and technology, we can see that never before in human history has the range of possibilities and limitations for achieving environmental peace and sustainable development been so wide. In the face of a panorama of almost unlimited technological development and an opulence in the developed world that permits uncontrollable waste on military expenditures and shameful destruction of natural resources, human misery continues. Like the loss of biodiversity, it is caused by the accelerated alteration of the habitats and ecosystems of the developing world. Parallel to this destruction, a national and international order with unjust and archaic socioeconomic and political systems persists, violating human dignity, environmental stability, and the sovereignty and economy of nations. This violation occurs despite the vast means for changing direction and maintaining options for development without destruction.

For Central America time is short; given the rhythm of environmental deterioration, the limitations on giving human beings their just value, and the backward step in the quality of life, the challenges cannot be postponed. Paradoxically, the pressing need to increase production is becoming greater today at the same time that the importance and urgency to conserve, *in order to continue* producing and existing, is growing. When resources are scarce and the organizational schemes and orientation of the economy do not favor making accurate and rapid decisions, there are no simple solutions. Nevertheless, everything points toward a new vision of the world: the regional conflicts, abysmal material inequalities, elevated population growth rates, rampant deforestation, loss of soils through erosion, predation of marine and coastal riches, growth of sprawling urban centers with their proliferation of slums and environmental contamination, irreparable loss of genetic material, overwhelming foreign debt, growing corruption, and the lethargy in consolidation of democratic regimes all demand a new order of things.

There is no doubt that the seeds for this change—contained as much in vision as in values—could originate in the new concept of the world with which the environmental movement has provided us. The reality of a finite world and the awareness of the insignificance of our planet within the infinite cosmos—as the space exploration of the 1960s showed us—have generated the image of the Earth as a spaceship. At the same time, this view has made us conscious that our destiny is linked to whatever happens to this fabulous space vehicle, a mere 5 million years old, that has permitted the almost magical evolution of its biological riches.

Our new awareness of this genetic treasure—as well as of our smallness and vulnerability—has generated a notion that the survival of humanity and of much of the life that we know today depends on human beings coexisting with nature and each other. In the face of this realization, the need for a shared responsibility could not be clearer.

It is no accident that, at the end of the 1960s and during the early 1970s, an environmental movement began that is now becoming impossible to contain. It congealed in the spring of 1970, a year after the first trip to the moon, when Earth Day was celebrated in several developed countries. Central America, despite its simplicity and relative underdevelopment, could not isolate itself from these currents. Hundreds of professionals from the region went to study in some of the centers of environmental ebullience of the time. Upon returning to our countries, we took up the environmental flag eager to reveal the grave condition of our unhealthy Planet Earth, and thus we began to organize the first activist movements in defense of the environment.

In 1974, with the support of international organizations, the First Central American Meeting for the Management of Natural and Cultural Resources took place, unquestionably a landmark event in the history of the regional movement surrounding environmental problems. Central America Day was one of the unanticipated, long-term results of this movement.

With the help of the World Conservation Union (IUCN), representatives from each of the region's nations have worked together on this book. That fact, together with the recent formation of a regional network of environmental organizations in Central America (REDES-CA), is eloquent testimony that environmental concern is generating new values of union between peoples and a vision of the future that contains the hope of survival and eco-solidarity, as it should, as much on the ecological plane as on the economic one.

The concrete results of the case studies described herein, the strengthening of nongovernmental organizations and the growing international support as well as the efforts to consolidate peace in Central America, are sources of optimism and hope for a promising future for the region. This future also depends on raising an environmental consciousness, improving living conditions for the popular sectors, getting support from the highest political levels, and on international solidarity in the ecological field.

We must remember that great deeds and monumental tasks cannot be fulfilled while we are tied to the past. Rather, we must be looking toward the future. This future will be ours if we can reverse the current process of self-destruction and marginalization by being ready, in solidarity, to wage a battle in favor of the environment and against poverty on this planet. We must fight for a desirable and sustainable future.

Index